P9-AGA-559

THE NEW MERMAIDS

# The Duchess of Malfi

# THE NEW MERMAIDS

*General Editors*
PHILIP BROCKBANK
BRIAN MORRIS

# The Duchess of Malfi

JOHN WEBSTER

*Edited by* ELIZABETH M. BRENNAN

*A New Mermaid*

A MERMAID DRAMABOOK

HILL AND WANG • NEW YORK

Manufactured in the United States of America
234567890

# CONTENTS

# TO
# MY PARENTS

# INTRODUCTION

## THE AUTHOR

VERY LITTLE IS known about John Webster. He was born free of the Merchant Taylors' Company, probably about 1580. There was a John Webster admitted to the Middle Temple on 1st August, 1598. If this were the dramatist, the fact might explain the many legal allusions in his plays and the inclusion of trial scenes in *The White Devil*, *The Devil's Law Case* and *Appius and Virginia*. Ben Jonson's are the only Elizabethan or Jacobean plays which contain more legal allusions than John Webster's.

The earliest records of Webster's employment as a playwright are found in the diary of the theatre manager and financier, Philip Henslowe. Among the payments which Henslowe noted in his diary in 1602 were those made to Webster, Munday, Middleton, Dekker, Chettle, Thomas Heywood and Wentworth Smith for their work on the plays *Caesar's Fall*, *Lady Jane* and *Christmas Comes but Once a Year*. It is thought that *The Famous History of Sir Thomas Wyatt* which was published in 1607 contains the contribution of Dekker and Webster to the second play. The other two plays, like so many mentioned in Henslowe's diary, including Webster's tragedy, *The Guise*, have been lost.

In 1604 Webster wrote the Induction for John Marston's *The Malcontent* and collaborated with Dekker on *Westward Ho!*. The following year they wrote *Northward Ho!*. Webster's first tragedy, *The White Devil*, was performed and published in 1612. Despite *The White Devil*'s apparently unsympathetic reception in the theatre, to which Webster refers in the preface to the first quarto, he seems to have lost no time in writing *The Duchess of Malfi*. An assiduous reader and borrower, Webster incorporated in his second tragedy some material which had only been published in 1612. Though the play cannot have been completed before late 1612, it must have been performed before 16th December, 1614 when William Ostler, the actor who first played Antonio Bologna, died.

Webster's elegy on the death of Prince Henry, *A Monumental Column*, was published in 1613. The sixth edition of Sir Thomas Overbury's *Characters* (1615) contained

thirty-two new 'characters', including that of 'An Excellent
Actor', which were probably contributed by Webster. The
dates of Webster's other extant works are uncertain. *The
Devil's Law Case* was performed about 1616. It is thought
that Webster collaborated with Middleton on *Anything for
a Quiet Life*, probably about 1621, and with Rowley and
possibly Thomas Heywood on *A Cure for a Cuckold* between 1624 and 1625. *Appius and Virginia*, first published
in 1654, may belong to the same period. The lost tragedy of
*The Guise* was written some time before 1623 and another
lost play, *The Late Murder of the Son upon the Mother, or
Keep the Widow Waking* which Webster wrote in collabora-
tion with Dekker, Ford and Rowley, was performed in
September, 1624. It has been suggested that *The Fair Maid
of the Inn*, published in the 1647 Folio of plays by Beaumont
and Fletcher, was written by Webster, Massinger and Ford.

Webster appears to have written no other plays, though
he is known to have composed a Lord Mayor's Pageant and
he wrote some occasional verses. He probably died in the
sixteen-thirties.

## EARLY PERFORMANCES OF WEBSTER'S PLAYS

*Caesar's Fall* AND *Lady Jane* were written for the Ad-
miral's Men and the Earl of Worcester's Men respectively.
The two citizen comedies, *Westward Ho!* and *Northward
Ho!* were written by Dekker and Webster for the company
of Paul's Boys who performed them in their private theatre.
Upon the accession of James I the Earl of Worcester's Men
changed their name to Queen Anne's Servants, or the
Queen's Men, and it was as the Queen's Men that they per-
formed *The White Devil*, *The Devil's Law Case* and *Keep the
Widow Waking* at the Red Bull, their theatre in Clerkenwell.

*The Duchess of Malfi* was acted by the King's Men, the
company which had performed *The Malcontent*. It was
presented both in their private theatre in Blackfriars and in
their public theatre, the Globe, between 1612 and 1614. It
was revived at least once before publication in 1623,[1] and
during the winter of 1630–1631 the King's Men presented
*The Duchess of Malfi* at the Cockpit theatre and also at
court. After the Restoration it was produced by the Duke's
Company and became one of their best stock tragedies. In
the early eighteenth century it was presented as *The Unfortunate Duchess of Malfi or The Unnatural Brothers* in the
Queen's theatre in the Haymarket.

[1] See Critical Notes, p. 103 below.

*Anything for a Quiet Life* was performed by the King's Men at the Blackfriars theatre in 1621.

## THE SOURCES OF THE PLAY

WEBSTER FOUND THE material for *The Duchess of Malfi*, as he had done that of *The White Devil*, in a true story of life in Italy in the century previous to his own. Giovanna d'Aragona had been married in 1490, when she was about twelve years old, to Alfonso Piccolomini, son and heir to the first Duke of Amalfi. Three years later he succeeded to the dukedom, but ruled only for five years before dying of gout. The Duchess, a girl of nineteen or twenty, was left with a daughter, Caterina. Her son was born posthumously in 1499 and succeeded to the dukedom which she ruled for him as regent. Despite French and Spanish invasions the state flourished, and the Duchess was able to pay off debts which had been incurred by her husband.

The Duchess of Amalfi had lived prosperously for some years before meeting Antonio Bologna who came of a reputable family and had been brought up at the court of Naples. As major-domo to Federico, the last Aragonian King of Naples, Antonio had followed his master into exile in France. Upon Federico's death in 1504 Antonio returned to Naples where he was offered the post of major-domo in the household of the young widowed Duchess, who was herself a member of the house of Aragon. The Duchess fell quickly and passionately in love with Antonio. Fearing the wrath of her brothers—Lodovico, who had resigned his title to become a Cardinal, and Carlo (Webster's Ferdinand) who had succeeded to his brother's title of Marquis of Gerace—the Duchess married her major-domo in secret, with her waiting-woman as sole witness of the ceremony.

Incredible as it may seem in life as in Webster's play, the marriage was successfully concealed for some years. The birth of the first child was undetected; but the birth of a second caused rumours which at last reached the ears of the Duchess' brothers, who set spies to watch her. Antonio took his two children to Ancona, leaving the Duchess, who was again pregnant, in her palace. Unbearably lonely, she soon found an excuse to set out with a great retinue for a pilgrimage to Loretto from whence she proceeded to join Antonio. Upon her arrival in Ancona she revealed her marriage to her household and declared that she would renounce her rank and title to live privately with her husband and their children. One of the astonished servants set out to inform the

Cardinal what had happened; the rest deserted her and returned to Amalfi.

At Ancona, where their third child was born, the Duchess and Antonio were allowed only a few months' peace before the Cardinal of Aragon put pressure on Cardinal Gonzaga, Legate of Ancona, to banish Antonio. Fortunately, Antonio had foreseen this, and had made preparations to take refuge with a friend in Siena. As soon as the decree of his banishment was issued—in the summer of 1511—Antonio set out with the Duchess and their children and so they escaped any possible attempts that might have been made to capture or murder them. The Cardinal continued to exert his influence against them and the head of the Signiory of Siena was persuaded by his brother, Cardinal Petrucci, to expel them from that city. This time Antonio and his family did not depart so quickly and on their way to Venice armed horsemen overtook them. By asserting that her brothers would not harm her in person the Duchess was able to persuade Antonio to escape with their eldest child, a boy of six or seven years of age, to Milan, where they arrived safely, probably in the later summer of 1512. There is no evidence to connect the Aragonian brothers with the death of the Duchess, but after being taken to her palace in Amalfi neither the Duchess nor her two youngest children nor her waiting-woman were ever seen again.

Antonio did not know what had happened to them. For over a year he lived in Milan, first under the protection of Silvio Savelli, and later in the households of the Marchese di Bitonto and Alfonso Visconti. Though his wife's brothers had confiscated his property in Naples, Antonio still hoped to appease them. Perhaps they held out promises of restoring the Duchess to him. Yet Antonio was continually being warned that his life was in danger. One person who gave him a warning was a man called Delio who had been told of Antonio's story by a Neapolitan friend. One day in October, 1513 Delio and a friend passed Antonio, who looked dismayed, with two servants on their way to mass at the church of S. Francesco. A few minutes later an uproar was heard and, looking back, Delio and his friend saw that Antonio had been stabbed to death by a Lombard captain called Daniele da Bozolo and three accomplices. All four escaped.

The diary of Giacomo the Notary, of Naples, records the stir caused by the Duchess' leaving her duchy to go on the pilgrimage to Loretto and by her subsequent revelation of the marriage to her major-domo. The Corona group of

manuscripts in the Biblioteca Nazionale in Naples contains
accounts of the Duchess' life which were originally collected
in the sixteenth century but which were subsequently
copied out and augmented by later writers up to the
eighteenth century. Behind these manuscripts lies the story
narrated as the twenty-sixth of the first part of Matteo
Bandello's *Novelle*, published in 1554. Though these
accounts contain more details of Neapolitan interest than
Bandello's novella, only one version is obviously indepen-
dent of his.[1]

The novella includes both material based on hearsay and
some imagined dialogue, but it is sufficiently accurate in
outline to warrant the assumption that, since Bandello
wrote sonnets under the name of Delio, he himself was the
Delio who had known Antonio Bologna and heard his story
in Milan; the Delio who had been a witness of Antonio's
murder.

Bandello relates the tragic story without moral comment,
but since his introduction decries murders which are moti-
vated by a desire to avenge wounded honour, a condemna-
tion of the Aragonian brothers is implicit. The French
writer François de Belleforest is more outspoken. At the
end of his account of the Duchess, the first story in his
second tome of *Histoires Tragiques*, the reader's sympathy
is with the murdered Duchess, the victim of her brothers'
cruelty; but in the course of his narration Belleforest exclaims continually against her. He presents her as a lascivious widow who is unable to live without a man and who
forgets her noble blood to run after a man far beneath her
station. Her feigned pilgrimage to Loretto is an execrable
impiety. This version, with its moral comment, was given
to English readers by William Painter in the *Second Tome
of the Palace of Pleasure* (1567). In *The Theatre of God's
Judgements* (1597) Thomas Beard takes an even less sympathetic view of the Duchess, treating the history of her
marriage under the heading 'Of whoredomes committed
vnder Colour of Marriage'. The tone of accounts of the
marriage given in George Whetstone's *An Heptameron of
Civil Discourses* (1582) and Edward Grimeston's *Admirable
and Memorable Histories* is condemnatory. Only in brief
references in H. C.'s *The Forest of Fancy* (1579) and Robert
Greene's *Gwydonius, the Card of Fancy* (1584) is the
Duchess' choice of husband commended.

[1] See Gunnar Boklund, *'The Duchess of Malfi' Sources, Themes,
Characters* (Cambridge, Mass., 1962), pp. 9–11.

Painter's version of Bandello was probably Webster's main source for the outline of *The Duchess of Malfi*. Some details of action, such as the mental torturing of the Duchess and the incorporation of the echo scene, and some parts of the dialogue are derived from the story of Musidorus and Pamela in Sidney's *Arcadia*. There are slight indications that Webster knew Bandello's novella in the original Italian, and he may possibly have read Lope da Vega's tragedy, *El Mayordomo de la Duquesa de Amalfi*, though it was not published till 1618.[1]

## WEBSTER'S TRAGEDY OF THE DUCHESS OF MALFI

THE MOST IMPORTANT difference between Webster's story of the Duchess of Malfi and that given by other writers lies in the attitude to the heroine. Webster's Duchess is not the wanton widow of Belleforest and Painter. Within the play itself the dramatist considers the possible charges against her and demonstrates how her life and death refute them, stressing her purity and integrity. Though Antonio's praise of her in the opening scene underlines her purity and her piety, these qualities are questioned by others because she lives in a society that is both corrupt and corrupting. Only in the fact that it is her own court which breeds corruption may any ambivalence of attitude to the Duchess be implicit; though the evidence of their characters almost certainly suggests that the Aragonian brothers constitute the 'curs'd example' which poisons their sister's court near the head.[2] Moreover, if their influence is sufficiently strong to limit the Duchess' freedom in marriage, there would not appear to be any possibility of her being able to exercise her ducal authority to rid the court of their unhealthy presence.

The evil with which the Duchess is supposed to be possessed is a projection of the evil in the minds of her brothers. Thus, when Ferdinand accuses her, both to her face and in her absence, of lust and wantonness, his words reveal the state of his own mind. His salaciousness is observed both in his conversation with courtiers (I,ii, 31–34)

---

[1] *Ibid.*, pp. 1–74.

[2] I,i, 13–15. For this interpretation 'near the head' is significant. As Regent the Duchess is the temporal head of the state; as the state's sovereign magistrate she is the source of its justice, her authority being derived from God. Complaints that she pays no attention to her duchy are frivolous. The fact that the play deals exclusively with her private life does not preclude the possibility of her leading an efficient public life whose activities lie outside the scope of Webster's concern in her tragedy.

and in the obscene allusion to women's preferences which his sister cannot mistake, though he tries to excuse it. Ferdinand questions whether her children—beggarly brats he calls them—were ever christened; but it is seen that one of the Duchess' last earthly concerns is that her daughter be brought up to pray. In the face of danger the Duchess is able to think and speak of Heaven; she accepts persecution as a necessary means of divine guidance (III,v, 73–78); she meets death kneeling, in an attitude of Christian humility. When life briefly revives in her strangled body Bosola sees her as a fair soul capable of leading him to salvation; when she is dead at last she epitomizes the

> . . . sacred innocence, that sweetly sleeps
> On turtles' feathers: . . .  (IV,ii, 349–50)

The Cardinal who complains that the Duchess makes religion her riding hood to keep her from the sun and tempest is the man who jokes obscenely with a mistress kept in his own household; the man who resigns his religious vestments for the accoutrements of war. The animality of Ferdinand's nature forces itself to the surface in the horrible form of lycanthropy. In contrast to the Duchess' last hours, those of her brothers reveal their consciousness of the hell that awaits them. Ferdinand declares in his madness that when he goes to hell he will take a bribe with him. The Cardinal is puzzled in a question about hell fire; troubled by the thing armed with a rake which seems to strike at him, threatening death and, at the same time, recalling the devils of the mystery plays who, armed with pitchforks, herded the bad souls into hell. Despite his military reputation, the Cardinal's death wants courage as much as it wants the kind of Christian stoicism displayed by his sister. His attitude in the face of death is no more dignified, no braver than Cariola's.

*The Duchess of Malfi*, like *The White Devil*, has the dramatic framework of the revenge play; but it contains fewer of the trappings of this type of drama which was popular on the English stage between 1588 and 1642. Two important actions, the Cardinal's investiture as a soldier and the Duchess' banishment, are performed in dumb show. There is no ghost, though the echo from the Duchess' tomb fulfils one of the functions of the ghost of revenge tragedy by warning a doomed man of his danger and, at the same time, revealing the unknown fact of its own death. The final action of the play, comprehending accidental or mistaken

murders, the poisoning of Julia, and the repeated stabbings
of the last scene, produces enough bloodshed and a number
of corpses to make the play comparable with the gory
tragedies of the 1590s. The trappings or conventions of
madness and the masque are combined in the dance of
madmen which forms part of the complicated mental torture to which the Duchess is subjected by Ferdinand.

Madness is incorporated in the action in other original
ways. Ferdinand's lycanthropy subtly serves a dual purpose.
Grounded in the animality of his nature, it forms part of
Webster's characterization. As lycanthropy was a recognized symptom of love-melancholy, it confirms Webster's
depiction of Ferdinand as a jealous lover of his sister.[1] In the
handling of the plot it enables the dramatist to make use of
an unpredictable element in the final conflict. The device of
madness is also skilfully treated in the character of the
Duchess. At the beginning of the play it is anticipated, not
only in some of Antonio's words (I,ii, 337–41), which also
adumbrate the later presentation of Ferdinand, but in the
striking lines which Cariola speaks at the conclusion of the
first act:

> Whether the spirit of greatness, or of woman
> Reign most in her, I know not, but it shows
> A fearful madness: I owe her much of pity. (I,ii, 417–9)

In the fourth act the Duchess' madness is more powerful as
a threat than in its brief and intermittent reality; there is no
doubt of her sanity when the moment of death approaches.

One of the themes of *The Duchess of Malfi* is that of
courtly reward, which Webster had previously explored in
*The White Devil*. In the earlier tragedy he opposes courtly
reward and courtly punishment; in *The Duchess of Malfi*
courtly reward is contrasted with courtly desert. As in *The
White Devil*, the theme is introduced in the opening scene
of the play in the words of a man who has received what
he considers unjust treatment; a man who is destined to be
the villain hired to murder the heroine.

In *The Duchess of Malfi* this villain, Bosola, is first
presented to the critical observation of Antonio and Delio

[1] See Lawrence Babb, *The Elizabethan Malady A Study of Melan-
cholia in English Literature from 1580 to 1642* (East Lansing, 1951),
pp. 136–7; Elizabeth M. Brennan, 'The Relationship between
Brother and Sister in the Plays of John Webster', *Modern Language
Review*, LVIII (1963), pp. 488–94.

as a discontented follower of the Cardinal. When Bosola
appeals to the Cardinal he is reproved for over-emphasizing
his own merit. After the Cardinal's departure the slighted
soldier exclaims on the life of a court dependant:

Who would rely upon these miserable dependences, in
expectation to be advanc'd tomorrow? What creature ever
fed worse, than hoping Tantalus; nor ever died any man
more fearfully, than he that hop'd for a pardon? There are
rewards for hawks, and dogs, when they have done us service;
but for a soldier, that hazards his limbs in a battle, nothing
but a kind of geometry is his last supportation.
*Delio.* Geometry?
*Bosola.* Ay, to hang in a fair pair of slings, take his latter
swing in the world, upon an honourable pair of crutches,
from hospital to hospital: fare ye well sir. And yet do not
you scorn us, for places in the court are but like beds in the
hospital, where this man's head lies at that man's foot, and
so lower and lower. (I,i, 54–68)[1]

Shortly afterwards Bosola is given employment. He is hired
by Ferdinand—but really by the Cardinal as well—to spy
on their sister. His hire is a sum of gold and employment as
provisor of the Duchess' horse. This is not, however, the
type of employment to appeal to Bosola of whom Antonio
has predicted that foul melancholy will poison his goodness.
Though Bosola is suspected of having committed a murder
at the Cardinal's instigation, he has the goodness or virtue
of a soldier: action and loyal service. His position as intelligencer, though profitable, is inactive. The court itself is
inactive, stagnant. Even Ferdinand complains, after
Antonio Bologna has been praised for skill in the tilt-yard:

. . . when shall we leave this sportive
action, and fall to action indeed? (I,ii, 9–10)

Inaction, stagnation and corruption are closely related. So
Bosola comments:

. . . what's my place?
The provisorship o'th' horse? say then my corruption
Grew out of horse dung. (I,ii, 206–8)

Yet in the play worth and virtue are recognized and
rewarded. The young Duchess of Malfi responds with love
to Antonio Bologna's nobleness of nature, and, though he
is her major-domo, she makes him, not an equal, but her
[1] *Cf. The White Devil*, ed. F. L. Lucas, III,i, 38–57; III,iii, 1–9.

lord in marriage.[1] That the worth of a lowly man should be
thus acknowledged is something which astonishes Bosola,
whose well-timed commendation of Antonio after the
latter's apparent dismissal betrays the Duchess into revealing the secret of her marriage. Bosola's exclamation of
wonder pleases the Duchess. Glad to have found (as she
thinks) an ally, proud to hear her husband praised, the
Duchess declares that she has had three children by him.
At this Bosola exclaims:

> Fortunate lady,
> For you have made your private nuptial bed
> The humble and fair seminary of peace.
> No question but many an unbenefic'd scholar
> Shall pray for you, for this deed, and rejoice
> That some preferment in the world can yet
> Arise from merit. The virgins of your land,
> That have no dowries, shall hope your example
> Will raise them to rich husbands. Should you want
> Soldiers, 'twould make the very Turks and Moors
> Turn Christians, and serve you for this act.
> Last, the neglected poets of your time,
> In honour of this trophy of a man,
> Rais'd by that curious engine, your white hand,
> Shall thank you in your grave for't; and make that
> More reverend than all the cabinets
> Of living princes. . . . (III,ii, 280–96)

This speech is one of the most dramatically ironic in the
play; for though won to admiration of the Duchess, Bosola
is powerless to prevent himself from betraying her. Ironic-
ally, the victim whom he is hired to destroy is a prince
worthier his service than her brothers. Yet Bosola's very
promise to keep her secret in his heart is a means of gaining
her confidence through which he may rise in his real master's
service. Thus it is Bosola who advises the Duchess to make
a feigned pilgrimage to Loretto and it is he who leads the
band of soldiers who overtake her after her flight from the
shrine into banishment.

It is Bosola's personal tragedy that, having sold his ser-
vices to the evil brothers, he is forced to be a destroyer of

[1] Here Webster alters the characterization of Antonio given by
Belleforest and Painter who show him deliberately calculating the
financial advantages of marriage with the Duchess. For a full
consideration of Webster's presentation of Antonio, see F. W.
Wadsworth, 'Webster's *Duchess of Malfi* in the Light of Some
Contemporary Ideas on Marriage and Remarriage', *Philological
Quarterly*, XXXV (1956), pp. 394–407 (especially pp. 401–7).

goodness that is personified in their sister. For Bosola is sensible of the qualities of the Duchess and he tries, in his own fashion, to bring her comfort. He has no physical comfort to offer her but, when she has lost all that means most in this world, Bosola prevents her from losing eternity. Mental affliction brings her to despair; to die in despair is to die denying the grace of God. Bosola's appearances in a variety of disguises are not further acts of torment; they are sympathetic attempts to make the Duchess rise from despair. As the tomb-maker he stresses the importance of the soul by reminding her of the frailty of the body. His message—of the life of the soul—is one of Christian comfort; and it is to this message that the Duchess responds with an assertion of her own integrity:

I am Duchess of Malfi still. (IV,ii, 139)

She is afraid neither of death nor of the manner of her death. She can say, sincerely,

. . . Tell my brothers
That I perceive death, now I am well awake,
Best gift is, they can give, or I can take. (IV,ii, 219–21)

At the moment of death her soul is prepared for Heaven.

The Duchess has said that she is awake; and her waking gives her a recognition of the reward of death: Heaven. After she is strangled Bosola claims his reward from Ferdinand. He is offered what Brachiano and Vittoria offer Flamineo in *The White Devil*: a bare pardon. Bosola therefore wakens from his 'golden dream' to the realization of his own damnation. Then the stirring of the Duchess gives him a tantalizing promise of salvation.

Return, fair soul, from darkness, and lead mine
Out of this sensible hell. (IV,ii, 336–7)

he cries; but the Duchess expires and Bosola is left to work out, not his own salvation, but his own damnation in the kind of action which he has long neglected.

The theme of courtly reward opposed to courtly desert is used by Webster to enforce the ironies of the final scene of the play. The Cardinal who had indirectly bought Bosola's life, in the sense of his life-work, tries vainly to buy his own life at Bosola's hands. Bosola comments on this reversal of position by referring to the Cardinal's presumed profession of Christianity and his real manifestation of corruption in the same breath:

> Thy prayers and proffers
> Are both unseasonable. (V,v, 15–16)

The Cardinal cries for mercy; but to extend mercy to him
would be an act of injustice. So Bosola reminds him:

> Pray, and be sudden: when thou kill'd'st thy sister,
> Thou took'st from Justice her most equal balance,
> And left her naught but her sword. (V,v, 38–40)

Though Bosola stabs the Cardinal twice, it is Ferdinand
who, in his madness, kills his brother and gives Bosola his
death-wound also. The Cardinal acknowledges the justice
of his own death, while Bosola reaches the climax of his
courtly service in rewarding Ferdinand for his iniquity. He
kills Ferdinand, rejoicing that

> . . . the last part of my life
> Hath done me best service. (V,v, 63–64)

Probably for the first time in his career, Bosola has stabbed
a villain instead of an innocent. But the Cardinal is not quite
dead. He has strength left to speak of Bosola's death in
terms which relate it to the reward that Bosola has been
seeking from him for so long:

> Thou hast thy payment too. (V,v, 73)

Bosola survives to explain to Roderigo the reason for the
deaths that have taken place with such swift violence. Signi-
ficantly, his final speech deals not with reward, but with
revenge: for revenge is both a human reward for injury and
an instrument of divine vengeance for sin. Revenge is
Bosola's reward to Ferdinand for neglected service and
neglected human nature.

The theme of courtly reward and desert, which appears
in other passages in the play besides those that have just
been considered, is important; but it is only one of many
themes that Webster examines. Some themes, suggested by
the action, are explicitly stated in sententiae and philosophic
utterances.[1] The significance of others is brought out by the
play's imagery. The most notable group of images is concerned with the idea of confinement, which is represented
as a prison or a trap. One of the most important statements
of this theme indicates that the soul is a prisoner of the body
which will only be liberated in death. The soul is like a

[1] Discussions of Webster's philosophy, particularly as it is expressed in the closing speeches of the play, are listed below, pp.
115–6.

caged bird, and the Duchess of Malfi is entrapped as men
catch birds, with nets and cunning practices.

Webster approaches this idea indirectly and subtly. In
hiring Bosola to spy on their sister, the Cardinal and Ferdinand are setting a trap; and as men trap wild creatures in
order to kill them, so the Duchess, if trapped, will be killed.
Ferdinand's apparent warning—

> . . . believe't,
> Your darkest actions: nay, your privat'st thoughts,
> Will come to light. (I,ii, 234–6)

—and the Cardinal's comment on secret marriage—

> The marriage night
> Is the entrance into some prison. (I,ii, 243–4)

—are not prophecies, but threats. Bosola's first task is to
discover her secrets; his second is to secure her imprisonment.

Bosola's intelligencing takes years to produce the required
results, but the threats have an immediate fulfilment in the
life of the Duchess which is unknown to her brothers. Their
determined wills and the atmosphere of her own poisoned
court limit the Duchess' activities. Her secret marriage is
literally confined within the walls of her chamber, and in this
sense her marriage night is the entrance to a prison. It is a
prison in another sense, too; for the Duchess' movements
and emotions are as restricted as those of a prisoner; she is
denied any liberty in marriage.

The wooing scene is shot through and through with a
variety of images which suggest, prophetically, not only
confinement, but madness and violent death.[1] Nevertheless,
a much happier instance of the image of confinement occurs
in the Duchess' reply to Antonio's question about her
brothers:

> Do not think of them:
> All discord, without this circumference,
> Is only to be pitied, and not fear'd. (I,ii, 383–5)

This may be interpreted as a reference to the wedding ring
that she has given Antonio, or to the confinement of the
wife's arms as she embraces her husband.

[1]See Critical Notes, p. 106 below. When the Duchess asks Heaven's
blessing on the 'sacred Gordian' it is to be remembered that the
Gordian knot was not untwined, but severed by a sword. Similarly,
the Duchess suggests that she and Antonio might lie with a naked
sword between them.

The idea of betrayal through some form of trapping is
present in Antonio's recognition, after the birth of his first
child, that Bosola is trying to undermine him. The concept
of something precious being confined in something frail,
parallel to that of the soul being imprisoned in the body, is
reflected in Ferdinand's exclamation:

> Foolish men,
> That e'er will trust their honour in a bark,
> Made of so slight, weak bulrush, as is woman,
> Apt every minute to sink it! (II,v, 33–36)

The carefully prepared trap catches the Duchess, but not
her husband. So Ferdinand alone, not relying on Bosola,[1]
goes to take them both in the Duchess' lodgings. Through
the operation of an aspect of his good nature which reveals
itself in good-natured teasing, Antonio has left his wife
alone. So the poniard which might have killed him is
presented by Ferdinand as a warning—or as a hint to
commit suicide—to Antonio's wife. The Duchess ignores
the hint. She plans to secure life and liberty first for her
husband, and then for herself and their children. In doing
this she rashly accepts Bosola's advice which is itself a snare.
Yet, though Bosola suggests a feigned pilgrimage, the
Duchess and her family do make their devotions at the
shrine. It is also at the shrine that her brother Cardinal
resigns his religious vestments and is accoutred as a soldier
before the Duchess and her family are banished; and in the
sight and hearing of pilgrims who comment on his cruel
bearing, the Cardinal vents his rage upon his sister by tearing
the wedding ring from her finger.

Having captured the Duchess in her flight Bosola seems
to take a delighted amusement in taunting her with the
question that reveals his own treachery:

> . . . I would have you tell me whether
> Is that note worse that frights the silly birds
> Out of the corn; or that which doth allure them
> To the nets? You have heark'ned to the last too much.
> (III,v, 98–101)

Yet Bosola is vizarded when he says this, so that his boast
loses its force and appears instead as a mysterious reflection
on an otherwise unknown plan of the Duchess. The idea of
the Duchess as a trapped bird is underlined by the way in

[1] In fact Ferdinand behaves as if he were a cuckold going to trap
his wife with a lover. See Elizabeth M. Brennan, *op. cit.*, p. 493.

which Ferdinand plays cruelly with her before her death. Immediately upon being captured she asks Bosola to what prison she must go, but he insists that she is not to be imprisoned; her brothers mean her safety and pity. The Duchess knows better:

> Pity!
> With such a pity men preserve alive
> Pheasants and quails, when they are not fat enough
> To be eaten. (III,v, 108–11)

Nevertheless, shortly afterwards the trapping net becomes a symbol of necessary evil which will reveal good: just as death is an evil which, at the Judgement, will reveal the good of the soul. This appears at the conclusion of the Duchess' fable of the Salmon and the Dogfish:

> 'O', quoth the Salmon, 'sister, be at peace:
> Thank Jupiter, we both have pass'd the Net,
> Our value never can be truly known,
> Till in the Fisher's basket we be shown;
> I'th' Market then my price may be the higher,
> Even when I am nearest to the Cook, and fire.
>
> (III,v, 133–38)

The use of capitals in the first quarto suggests a parabolic interpretation of this apparently simple fable: the Fisher is God; the gathering in of the fishes is a harvest at which not wheat and tares, but good and bad fish are to be judged; the Market is the Judgement; the Cook is another symbol for God; the fire represents hell fire: at the Judgement one is as close to hell as to the joys of heaven. The whole passage is a comment on the difference between divine and human estimation of worth and thus it is related to the theme of reward and desert; the attitude of the Dogfish to rank is related to the play's comments on princes and their courts.

Images of imprisonment occur most frequently in the fourth act. In her own palace the Duchess is subjected to treatment which suggests that she is imprisoned as a punishment and restrained because she is mad. The question of whether or not she is really imprisoned is reiterated. Cariola assures her that she will live 'to shake this durance off', but the Duchess' mind turns again to contemplate the imprisoned bird: which is how Bosola has taught her to think of herself:

> The robin red-breast and the nightingale
> Never live long in cages. (IV,ii, 13–14)

The birds she mentions are such as she had earlier envied
for their ability to

> . . . choose their mates,
> And carol their sweet pleasures to the spring.
> (III,v, 19–20)

The idea of imprisonment is most forcefully expressed in
the imagery of Bosola's words to the Duchess:

Thou art a box of worm seed, at best, but a salvatory of green
mummy: what's this flesh? a little cruded milk, fantastical
puff-paste: our bodies are weaker than those paper prisons
boys use to keep flies in: more contemptible; since ours is to
preserve earth-worms: didst thou ever see a lark in a cage?
such is the soul in the body: this world is like her little turf
of grass, and the heaven o'er our heads, like her looking-glass,
only gives us a miserable knowledge of the small compass of
our prison. (IV,ii, 123–31)

The final symbol of the Duchess of Malfi's confinement is
the coffin itself: what Bosola calls her 'last presence chamber'. Her own last thought is of a confinement that leads
immediately to liberty. So she halts her executioners for an
instant:

> Yet stay, heaven gates are not so highly arch'd
> As princes' palaces: they that enter there
> Must go upon their knees. (IV,ii, 228–30)

'Strait is the gate and narrow is the way.' The implied contrast is with the space, the broad way that leads to perdition.

Though the Duchess dies in the fourth act, the image
which has hitherto been so closely associated with her
remains. Bosola, who once ensnared the Duchess for her
brothers, is able to confine the Cardinal to the room in
which the Duchess' death is to be avenged. So caught, the
Cardinal cries,

> Shall I die like a leveret
> Without any resistance? (V,v, 44–45)

Many other groups of images in the play deserve careful
attention. Those associated with corruption are offensive to
the senses: Bosola says that his preferment grew out of
horse dung; he tells the Duchess that the apricocks were
ripened in dung, implying that their flavour is tainted. In
the face of suffering, thinking that her husband and children
are dead, the Duchess exclaims,

> There is not between heaven and earth one wish
> I stay for after this: it wastes me more,

Than were't my picture, fashion'd out of wax,
Stuck with a magical needle, and then buried
In some foul dunghill: . . . (IV,i, 61–65)

Physical corruption is suggested by diseases such as leprosy
and consumption; Bosola is described as 'the only court-
gall'. There are frequent references to poison, and some to
magic and witchcraft. Images of brightness are suggested
by glass and by diamonds.

What would it pleasure me, to have my throat cut
With diamonds? . . . (IV,ii, 212–13)

asks the Duchess in one of her finest speeches before death;
while her brother Ferdinand dies proclaiming:

*Whether we fall by ambition, blood, or lust,*
*Like diamonds we are cut with our own dust.*
(V,v, 71–72)

Ferdinand, in his lycanthropy, personifies part of the animal
imagery of the play. The inanimate forces of nature, too, are
present, in references to storm and tempest. The language
of the madmen's scene reflects the corruption of the total
world of the play, while images drawn from the theatre
produce a distancing effect upon the action.

The imagery of *The Duchess of Malfi* constantly suggests
a series of contrasts and parallels: between light and darkness; health and sickness; sanity and insanity; life and
death. Webster presents other contrasts by different means.
Antonio is skilled in the tilt-yard and speaks in praise of
good horsemanship; Bosola becomes provisor of the
Duchess' horse. Thus an ironic parallel between them is
implied. The jesting of the Duchess and Antonio as they
prepare for bed is echoed in some of the words Bosola
speaks to her before her murder. Similarly, the Duchess'
first wooing of Antonio is paralleled to and contrasted with
Julia's wooing of Bosola; the Duchess' secret, but fruitful
marriage to Antonio contrasts with the openly scorned,
sterile, 'conventional' union of Julia with the old courtier
Castruchio.

Such contrasts are related to a conflict at the heart of the
play: the conflict between appearance and reality. This is
epitomized in the Duchess from the moment when, having
told her brothers that she will never marry, she immediately
turns to complete her plan of marrying Antonio; but,
indeed, this conflict is present in each of the major characters. The brothers who should love the Duchess are her

most cruel enémies; the husband who should give her
strength has to take courage from her example. The most
complicated presentation is found in Bosola, in whom it is
made visible through the use of disguises, though they are
in fact less important than the invisible disguising of his
true nature at the beginning of the play, and his conversion,
after the death of the Duchess, at the end.

The death of the Duchess suggests a paradox: the darkness of evil extinguishes the light of good, but only to
liberate the good, fair soul from its paper prison and its
cage into the light of eternity. It is Bosola who is left in
'this sensible hell' where, despite conversion, he is unable
to prevent himself from murdering goodness.

Some themes in *The Duchess of Malfi* echo ideas that
were explored in *The White Devil*. These are the ideas
associated with the corruption of princely courts and of
great men. Both tragedies also provide, through their action,
the opportunity of pondering on the different ways in which
men and women face death.

An examination of themes and images in *The Duchess of
Malfi* provides one method of interpreting its meaning; a
study of the characters' philosophy constitutes another.
Yet neither method provides a means of answering the
question which the story itself so forcibly presents: *Why*
was the Duchess of Malfi murdered? Many answers to the
question have been given, both in the play itself and by
modern commentators on it, no less than by the early
narrators of her history. She has been accused of a variety
of misdemeanours: marrying outside the church; jesting
with religion; marrying beneath her station; succumbing to
lust. It must be admitted that she does literally marry outside the church; that she calls Cariola a 'superstitious
fool' for objecting to a feigned pilgrimage; and that the
Duchess herself recognizes that simple virtue should not be
forced into devious paths; only unjust actions should wear
the masks and curtains which she and her husband have to
adopt. It is the evil will of her brothers—one of them a
Cardinal—that forces her to a secret marriage which is not
illegal. The Duchess later speaks of it as a sacrament of the
church.[1] Cariola tries to fend off death with the cry that she
has not been to confession for two years; if she dies now she
is damned. In the Duchess' calm preparation for the next
world there is the implication that—by contrast—she is in a

[1] IV,i, 39: see Critical Notes, p. 111 below. Antonio also speaks of
marriage as a sacrament. (I,ii, 305).

state of grace. So she appears to Bosola as 'sacred innocence'; and yet it is after this that Webster shows how Julia's wooing of Bosola echoes the Duchess' swift wooing of Antonio.[1]

To some critics the power of the threat of evil to the goodness of the Duchess lies in its unspecified horror. The Aragonian brothers have no valid reason for killing her. Within the play they both produce reasons for their deeds, but these need to be carefully examined. Webster's characterization of Ferdinand suggests that incestuous love of the Duchess explains his behaviour, but there is no such explanation for the Cardinal's share in her death. Other questions which deserve attention concern whether the brothers are realistically or symbolically represented; why Ferdinand appears to be the Cardinal's twin; what significance there is in Webster's making Ferdinand the Duchess' twin, and her junior.

John Webster's poetry has long been appreciated and its dramatic power recognized. One of the most interesting aspects of his poetry is the method of its composition; for its fine texture is woven from a mass of ideas, many of them borrowed from other writers, and today no appreciation of Webster can be considered complete that does not make use of the information presented in Professor R. W. Dent's full and excellent study, *John Webster's Borrowing* (Berkeley and Los Angeles, 1960). Shakespeare, Jonson, Chapman and Marston all made use of printed sources when writing their plays; but none was so indebted to his reading in general or to his commonplace book in particular as John Webster. An examination of his borrowing does not reveal an unimaginative mind, but an original mind engaged in an unique method of poetic and dramatic composition. The knowledge that there are discoverable sources for many lines of Webster's most striking speeches does not preclude admiration of his art; rather, it shifts the focus of attention from the ideas expressed to the method of expression.

John Webster's two great tragedies are rich in poetry and dramatic imagery; they contain discussions of themes which are of permanent moral significance, and they also present the audience with questions whose answers are still elusive. In differing degrees the heroines of both plays command

[1] There are not only ambiguities of character to be considered, but some inconsistencies of detail in the execution of plot as well as character: see Clifford Leech, *Webster: The Duchess of Malfi* (1963), pp. 48–49.

respect for their courage; sympathy for their human weakness; compassion for their inhuman treatment at the hands
of others. For these reasons *The White Devil* and *The
Duchess of Malfi* are ranked second to Shakespeare's
tragedies on the Jacobean stage.

## NOTE ON THE TEXT

THIS EDITION OF *The Duchess of Malfi* is based on the text
of the first quarto (British Museum copies: 644.f.72 and
Ashley 2207) which has been collated with the later quartos
and the principal modern editions, and emended where
necessary. Q1 (1623) is the most authoritative. Q2 (1640) is
based on Q1, with some emendations and some mistakes.
Q3 (1678), based on Q2, corrects some of the mistakes and
introduces others. Q4 is an abbreviated and altered version
of the play, published in 1708 as *The Unfortunate Dutchess
of Malfy or The Unnatural Brothers*. The whole of Act III,
Scene iv, is omitted; many speeches are cut or rephrased.
Where the text does follow that of the previous quartos it is
seen to be based on Q3 with some corrections made by
reference to Q1. If the compositor was unable to decide
between the conflicting readings of earlier quartos he simply
rephrased the line or speech where he found the difficulty.
(See collation of II,ii, 1; II,iv, 66.) On the other hand,
Q4 contains some sensible corrections of errors in the three
previous quartos. (See collation of II,i, 124, 131; III,ii, 79,
90; IV,i, 89.) This edition does not give a complete collation
of the quartos: only those variants which alter or emend the
Q1 text are considered. Major variants are recorded in the
page notes; minor variants are noted in the Textual
Appendix—A. Turned letters and minor variations in ortho-
graphy are not included.[1]

The spelling of the Q1 text has been modernized and
where two or more forms of spelling are found (as, for
example, *ore* and *o'er*, —*de* and —*'d, taine, ta'en* and *tane*)
the commonest form is used throughout (*o'er*, —*'d* and
*tane*).

The careful research of Dr. J. R. Brown has shown that
the text of Q1 was set up by two compositors who worked
from a manuscript that had probably been copied out by
the professional scribe, Ralph Crane. Compositor A followed the manuscript closely and, in order to reproduce

[1] Thus the collation of IV,ii, 162, for example, is abbreviated from a
full collation which would read: *charnel* ed. (Q1 charnell; Q2
chamell; Q3 chamel; Q4 Charnel).

the large number of colons and semicolons which are
typical of Crane's usage, he often took more than his fair
share of the available supply of these. As a result, compositor B had to replace some of the manuscript's colons and
semicolons with commas. The punctuation of this edition
is based on compositor A's practice in the Q1 text. An
attempt has been made to make passages set up by compositor B correspond in punctuation to those set up by
compositor A. Some idiosyncrasies and ambiguities of the
Q1 punctuation—the use of colons for stops, the placing
of commas between subject and verb, the use of brackets for
phrases in parentheses—have been removed where they
might otherwise prove distracting to a modern reader. Q1
question marks have been changed to exclamation marks
where the change is appropriate and interrupted speeches
(indicated in Q1 by commas or colons) are marked by
dashes; but the number of exclamation marks and dashes
introduced in the text has been kept as low as possible.
Speech-prefixes have been expanded throughout the text.

All the stage directions of Q1, except some 'block entries'
(see Textual Appendix-A, pp. 117-8 below), are incorporated
in the text. If they interrupt speech they are enclosed in
round brackets. Editorial additions to the stage directions
are indicated by square brackets.

## ACKNOWLEDGEMENTS

IN THE PREPARATION of this edition I am indebted to those
previous editors whose names are listed in the Textual
Appendix, p. 117 below. In particular I should like to
acknowledge the debts that I owe to F. L. Lucas's edition
of Webster; to Dr. J. R. Brown's bibliographical studies
of the play, and to the critical work of Dr. Gunnar Boklund
and Professor Clifford Leech. I am also grateful to the
General Editor of the Series, Professor Philip Brockbank,
for his sympathetic criticism and guidance.

ELIZABETH M. BRENNAN

*University College of North Wales,*
*Bangor, Caernarvonshire.*

*November* 1963

# FURTHER READING

The following books and articles have made valuable contributions to the study of John Webster and *The Duchess of Malfi*:

Charles Lamb, *Specimens of English Dramatic Poets, who lived about the Time of Shakespear: with notes* (1808).

E. E. Stoll, *John Webster: The Periods of His Work as Determined by His Relations to the Drama of His Day* (Boston, Mass., 1905).

Rupert Brooke, *John Webster and The Elizabethan Drama* (1916).

P. Haworth, *English Hymns and Ballads and Other Studies in Popular Literature* (Oxford, 1927).

M. C. Bradbrook, *Themes and Conventions of Elizabethan Tragedy* (Cambridge, 1935).

Una Ellis-Fermor, *The Jacobean Drama* (1936).

S. A. Tannenbaum, *Elizabethan Bibliographies: John Webster* (New York, 1941).

M. C. Bradbrook, 'Two Notes upon Webster', *Modern Language Review*, XLII (1947), 281–94.

M. E. Prior, *The Language of Tragedy* (New York, 1947).

Clifford Leech, *John Webster: A Critical Study* (1951).

Gabriele Baldini, *John Webster e il linguaggio della tragedia* (Rome, 1953).

J. R. Brown, 'The Printing of John Webster's Plays'—3 parts: *Studies in Bibliography* VI, 117–140; VIII, 113–128; XV, 57–69, (1954, 1956, 1962).

Travis Bogard, *The Tragic Satire of John Webster* (Berkeley and Los Angeles, 1955).

Hereward T. Price, 'The Function of Imagery in John Webster', *Publications of the Modern Language Association of America*, LXX (1955), 717–39.

C. W. Davies, 'The Structure of *The Duchess of Malfi* An Approach', *English* XII (1958), 89–93.

J. R. Mulryne, ' "The White Devil" and "The Duchess of Malfi" ', *Stratford-upon-Avon Studies 1: Jacobean Theatre* (1960), pp. 201–25.

R. W. Dent, *John Webster's Borrowing* (Berkeley and Los Angeles, 1960)

Gunnar Boklund, '*The Duchess of Malfi*' *Sources, Themes, Characters* (Cambridge, Mass., 1962).

Clifford Leech, *John Webster: 'The Duchess of Malfi*' (1963).

Other books and articles, which throw light on particular passages of the play, are listed in the Critical Notes under the passages concerned.

# THE
# TRAGEDY

## OF THE DVTCHESSE
## Of Malfy.

*As it was Presented priuatly, at the Black-*
*Friers; and publiquely at the Globe, By the*
Kings Maiesties Seruants.

The perfect and exact Coppy, with diuerse
*things Printed, that the length of the Play would*
not beare in the Presentment.

## VVritten by *John Webster.*

Hora.——*Si quid*——
——*Candidus Imperti si non his vtere mecum.*

## LONDON:

Printed by NICHOLAS OKES, for IOHN
WATERSON, and are to be sold at the
signe of the Crowne, in *Paules*
Church-yard, *1623*.

12–13 *Si quid . . . mecum:* 'If you know wiser precepts than these,
be kind and tell me; if not, practise mine with me.' Horace,
*Epistles,* I,vi, 67–8

# [DRAMATIS PERSONÆ]

[*Bosola*, gentleman of the horse
*Ferdinand*, Duke of Calabria
*Cardinal*, his brother
*Antonio*, steward of the Duchess' household
*Delio*, his friend.
*Forobosco*
*Malateste*, a Count.
*The Marquis of PESCARA.*
*Silvio*, a Lord.
*Castruchio*, an old Lord.
*Roderigo* }
*Grisolan* }  Lords.
*The Duchess*
*Cariola*, her woman.
*Julia*, wife to Castruchio and mistress to the Cardinal.
*The DOCTOR*
*Court Officers*
The several mad men, including: *Astrologer, Tailor, Priest,*
                                  *Doctor.*

*Old Lady*
*Three young children*
*Two pilgrims*
*Attendants, Ladies, Executioners.*]

*To the Right Honourable* GEORGE HARDING, BARON
BERKELEY, *of Berkeley Castle and Knight of the Order
of the Bath to the illustrious Prince* CHARLES.

My Noble Lord,
5    That I may present my excuse why, (being a stranger to
your Lordship) I offer this poem to your patronage, I
plead this warrant; men, who never saw the sea, yet desire
to behold that regiment of waters, choose some eminent river
to guide them thither; and make that as it were, their
10   conduct, or postilion. By the like ingenious means has
your fame arrived at my knowledge, receiving it from some
of worth, who both in contemplation, and practice, owe to
your Honour their clearest service. I do not altogether look
up at your title: The ancientest nobility, being but a relic of
15   time past, and the truest honour indeed being for a man to
confer honour on himself, which your learning strives to
propagate, and shall make you arrive at the dignity of a
great example. I am confident this work is not unworthy your
Honour's perusal for by such poems as this, poets have kissed
20   the hands of great princes, and drawn their gentle eyes to
look down upon their sheets of paper, when the poets themselves were bound up in their winding sheets. The like
courtesy from your Lordship, shall make you live in your
grave, and laurel spring out of it; when the ignorant scorners
25   of the Muses (that like worms in libraries, seem to live only,
to destroy learning) shall wither, neglected and forgotten.
This work and myself I humbly present to your approved
censure. It being the utmost of my wishes, to have your
honourable self my weighty and perspicuous comment:
30   which grace so done me, shall ever be acknowledged
By your Lordship's
in all duty and
observance,
John Webster.

10 *conduct* conductor
13 *clearest* most complete, absolute
14 *ancientest* ed. (Q1 ancien'st); *relic* ed. (Q1 rellique)
27–28 *approved censure* tried judgement

*In the just worth, of that well deserver*
*MR. JOHN WEBSTER, and upon this*
*masterpiece of tragedy.*

In this thou imitat'st one rich, and wise,
That sees his good deeds done before he dies;                    5
As he by works, thou by this work of fame,
Hast well provided for thy living name;
To trust to others' honourings, is worth's crime,
Thy monument is rais'd in thy life time;
And 'tis most just; for every worthy man                        10
Is his own marble; and his merit can
Cut him to any figure, and express
More art, than Death's cathedral palaces,
Where royal ashes keep their court: thy note
Be ever plainness, 'tis the richest coat:                       15
Thy epitaph only the title be,
Write, *Duchess*, that will fetch a tear for thee,
For who e'er saw this *Duchess* live, and die,
That could get off under a bleeding eye?


In Tragædiam.                                                    20
Ut lux ex tenebris ictu percussa tonantis;
Illa, (ruina malis) claris sit vita poetis.
                                Thomas Middletonus,
                                    Poëta & Chron:
                                    Londinensis.               25

20-22 To Tragedy.
    As light is struck from darkness at the blow of the thunderer,
    May it (ruin to the evil) be life to famous poets.
24-25 *Chron: Londinensis* Chronologer of London. (Middleton
    was appointed City Chronologer in 1620)

*To his friend* Mr John Webster
*Upon his* Duchess
of Malfi.

I never saw thy Duchess, till the day,
That she was lively body'd in thy play;
Howe'er she answer'd her low-rated love,
Her brothers' anger did so fatal prove,
Yet my opinion is, she might speak more;
But never (in her life) so well before.
                                    WIL: ROWLEY. .

*To the reader of the author,*
*and his* Duchess of Malfi

Crown him a poet, whom nor Rome, nor Greece,
Transcend in all theirs, for a masterpiece:
In which, whiles words and matter change, and men
Act one another; he, from whose clear pen
They all took life, to memory hath lent
A lasting fame, to raise his monument.
                                    JOHN FORD

5 *body'd* embodied
6 *answer'd* justified
16 *clear* pure

## Act I, Scene i

*[Enter* ANTONIO *and* DELIO.]

*Delio.* You are welcome to your country, dear Antonio,
You have been long in France, and you return
A very formal Frenchman, in your habit.
How do you like the French court?
  *Antonio.*     I admire it;
In seeking to reduce both State and people    5
To a fix'd order, their judicious King
Begins at home. Quits first his royal palace
Of flatt'ring sycophants, of dissolute,
And infamous persons, which he sweetly terms
His Master's master-piece, the work of Heaven,   10
Consid'ring duly, that a Prince's court
Is like a common fountain, whence should flow
Pure silver-drops in general. But if't chance
Some curs'd example poison't near the head,
*Death and diseases through the whole land spread.*  15
And what is't makes this blessed government,
But a most provident Council, who dare freely
Inform him, the corruption of the times?
Though some o'th' court hold it presumption
To instruct Princes what they ought to do,    20
It is a noble duty to inform them
What they ought to foresee. Here comes Bosola

*[Enter* BOSOLA]

The only court-gall: yet I observe his railing
Is not for simple love of piety:
Indeed he rails at those things which he wants,  25
Would be as lecherous, covetous, or proud,

Act I, Scene i and 15: see Textual Appendix, p. 117 below.
3 *habit* dress      6 *their* Q3, Q4 (Q1, Q2 there)
7 *Quits* rids      13 *in general* everywhere
18 *Inform him, the* inform him [about] the . . .
23 *court-gall* court sore-spot; as Lucas indicates, bitterness is
  also implicit.

Bloody, or envious, as any man,
If he had means to be so. Here's the Cardinal.
[*Enter* CARDINAL.]
    *Bosola.* I do haunt you still.
30    *Cardinal.* So.
    *Bosola.* I have done you better service than to be slighted
thus. Miserable age, where only the reward of doing well,
is the doing of it!
    *Cardinal.* You enforce your merit too much.
35    *Bosola.* I fell into the galleys in your service, where, for
two years together, I wore two towels instead of a shirt,
with a knot on the shoulder, after the fashion of a Roman
mantle. Slighted thus? I will thrive some way: blackbirds
fatten best in hard weather: why not I, in these dog days?
40    *Cardinal.* Would you could become honest,—
    *Bosola.* With all your divinity, do but direct me the way
to it. I have known many travel far for it, and yet return
as arrant knaves, as they went forth; because they carried
themselves always along with them. [*Exit* CARDINAL] Are
45    you gone? Some fellows, they say, are possessed with the
devil, but this great fellow were able to possess the greatest
devil, and make him worse.
    *Antonio.* He hath denied thee some suit?
    *Bosola.* He and his brother are like plum trees, that grow
50    crooked over standing pools, they are rich, and o'erladen
with fruit, but none but crows, pies, and caterpillars feed
on them. Could I be one of their flatt'ring panders, I would
hang on their ears like a horse-leech, till I were full, and
then drop off. I pray leave me. Who would rely upon these
55    miserable dependences, in expectation to be advanc'd
tomorrow? What creature ever fed worse, than hoping
Tantalus; nor ever died any man more fearfully, than he
that hop'd for a pardon? There are rewards for hawks, and
dogs, when they have done us service; but for a soldier, that
60    hazards his limbs in a battle, nothing but a kind of geometry is his last supportation.

32 *only the reward* the only reward
34 *enforce* urge, emphasize
39 *dog days* evil or unhealthy times, associated with hot weather
           when Sirius, the dog-star, is high in the sky
50 *standing pools* stagnant pools              51 *pies* magpies
55 *dependences* appointments in reversion
59 *dogs, when* Q2, Q3, Q4 (Q1 dogs, and when)
60-61 *a kind of geometry* hanging awkwardly and stiffly: see
           Critical Notes.

*Delio.* Geometry?

*Bosola.* Ay, to hang in a fair pair of slings, take his latter
swing in the world, upon an honourable pair of crutches,
from hospital to hospital: fare ye well sir. And yet do not          65
you scorn us, for places in the court are but like beds in the
hospital, where this man's head lies at that man's foot, and
so lower and lower.                              [*Exit* BOSOLA.

*Delio.* I knew this fellow seven years in the galleys,
For a notorious murther, and 'twas thought                          70
The Cardinal suborn'd it: he was releas'd
By the French general, Gaston de Foix
When he recover'd Naples.

*Antonio.*                    'Tis great pity
He should be thus neglected, I have heard
He's very valiant. This foul melancholy                              75
Will poison all his goodness, for, I'll tell you,
If too immoderate sleep be truly said
To be an inward rust unto the soul;
It then doth follow want of action
Breeds all black malcontents, and their close rearing,               80
Like moths in cloth, do hurt for want of wearing.


## Scene ii

[*Enter* CASTRUCHIO, SILVIO, RODERIGO *and* GRISOLAN.]

*Delio.* The presence 'gins to fill. You promis'd me
To make me the partaker of the natures
Of some of your great courtiers.

*Antonio.*                    The Lord Cardinal's
And other strangers', that are now in court?
I shall. Here comes the great Calabrian Duke.                         5

[*Enter* FERDINAND.]

*Ferdinand.* Who took the ring oft'nest?

*Silvio.* Antonio Bologna, my lord.

*Ferdinand.* Our sister Duchess' great master of her household? Give him the jewel: when shall we leave this sportive
action, and fall to action indeed?                                   10

70 *murther* Q1, Q2 (Q3, Q4 murtherer)
72 *Gaston de Foix* Q4 (Q1 Foux, Q2 Foyx, Q3 Fox) [lived 1489–
     1512]
Scene ii: see Textual Appendix—A.
1 *presence* presence, or audience chamber
6 *took the ring*, i.e. in jousting

*Castruchio.* Methinks, my lord, you should not desire to go to war, in person.

*Ferdinand [aside].* Now, for some gravity: why, my lord?

*Castruchio.* It is fitting a soldier arise to be a prince, but
15 not necessary a prince descend to be a captain!

*Ferdinand.* No?

*Castruchio.* No, my lord, he were far better do it by a deputy.

*Ferdinand.* Why should he not as well sleep, or eat, by a
20 deputy? This might take idle, offensive, and base office from him, whereas the other deprives him of honour.

*Castruchio.* Believe my experience: that realm is never long in quiet, where the ruler is a soldier.

*Ferdinand.* Thou told'st me thy wife could not endure
25 fighting.

*Castruchio.* True, my lord.

*Ferdinand.* And of a jest she broke, of a captain she met full of wounds: I have forgot it.

*Castruchio.* She told him, my lord, he was a pitiful fellow,
30 to lie, like the children of Ismael, all in tents.

*Ferdinand.* Why, there's a wit were able to undo all the chirurgeons o' the city, for although gallants should quarrel, and had drawn their weapons, and were ready to go to it; yet her persuasions would make them put up.

35 *Castruchio.* That she would, my lord.
How do you like my Spanish jennet?

*Roderigo.* He is all fire.

*Ferdinand.* I am of Pliny's opinion, I think he was begot by the wind; he runs as if he were ballass'd with quick-
40 silver.

*Silvio.* True, my lord, he reels from the tilt often.

*Roderigo* and *Grisolan.* Ha, ha, ha!

*Ferdinand.* Why do you laugh? Methinks you that are courtiers should be my touchwood, take fire when I give
45 fire; that is, laugh when I laugh, were the subject never so witty,—

*Castruchio.* True, my lord, I myself have heard a very

---

11 *should not desire* Q1, Q4 (Q2, Q3 should desire)
27 *jest she broke, of* joke she cracked about
30 *children of Ismael,* see Critical Notes; *tents* usual meaning; dressings for wounds
32 *chirurgeons* surgeons          34 *put up* sheathe their weapons
36 *jennet* a small Spanish horse   39 *ballass'd* ballasted
41 *reels from the tilt* jibs and refuses to run at the ring
44 *touchwood* tinder

good jest, and have scorn'd to seem to have so silly a wit, as
to understand it.

*Ferdinand.* But I can laugh at your fool, my lord.          50

*Castruchio.* He cannot speak, you know, but he makes
faces; my lady cannot abide him.

*Ferdinand.* No?

*Castruchio.* Nor endure to be in merry company: for she
says too much laughing, and too much company, fills her          55
too full of the wrinkle.

*Ferdinand.* I would then have a mathematical instrument
made for her face, that she might not laugh out of compass.
I shall shortly visit you at Milan, Lord Silvio.

*Silvio.* Your Grace shall arrive most welcome.          60

*Ferdinand.* You are a good horseman, Antonio; you have
excellent riders in France, what do you think of good
horsemanship?

*Antonio.* Nobly, my lord: as out of the Grecian horse
issued many famous princes: so out of brave horsemanship,          65
arise the first sparks of growing resolution, that raise the
mind to noble action.

*Ferdinand.* You have bespoke it worthily.

[ *Enter* DUCHESS, CARDINAL, CARIOLA *and* JULIA.]

*Silvio.* Your brother, the Lord Cardinal, and sister
Duchess.          70

*Cardinal.* Are the galleys come about?

*Grisolan.* They are, my lord.

*Ferdinand.* Here's the Lord Silvio, is come to take his
leave.

*Delio* [*aside to* ANTONIO]. Now sir, your promise: what's          75
that Cardinal? I mean his temper? They say he's a brave
fellow, will play his five thousand crowns at tennis, dance,
court ladies, and one that hath fought single combats.

*Antonio.* Some such flashes superficially hang on him, for
form: but observe his inward character: he is a melancholy          80
churchman. The spring in his face is nothing but the engen-
d'ring of toads: where he is jealous of any man, he lays
worse plots for them, than ever was impos'd on Hercules:
for he strews in his way flatterers, panders, intelligencers,

48 *silly* simple                    56 *wrinkle* crease; moral blemish
58 *out of compass* beyond the bounds of moderation
71 *come about* come round in the opposite direction, i.e. returned
       to port
79 *flashes* examples of ostentatious display
81 *spring* i.e. of water
84 *flatterers* Q3, Q4 (Q1, Q2 flatters); *intelligencers* spies, informers

85 atheists: and a thousand such political monsters: he
should have been Pope: but instead of coming to it by the
primitive decency of the Church, he did bestow bribes, so
largely, and so impudently, as if he would have carried it
away without Heaven's knowledge. Some good he hath done.
    *Delio.* You have given too much of him: what's his
90                                           brother?
    *Antonio.* The Duke there? a most perverse and turbulent
                                                nature;
What appears in him mirth, is merely outside,
If he laugh heartily, it is to laugh
All honesty out of fashion.
    *Delio.*               Twins?
    *Antonio.*               In quality:
95 He speaks with others' tongues, and hears men's suits
With others' ears: will seem to sleep o'th' bench
Only to entrap offenders in their answers;
Dooms men to death by information,
Rewards, by hearsay.
    *Delio.*           Then the law to him
100 Is like a foul black cobweb to a spider,
He makes it his dwelling, and a prison
To entangle those shall feed him.
    *Antonio.*               Most true:
He nev'r pays debts, unless they be shrewd turns,
And those he will confess, that he doth owe.
105 Last: for his brother, there, the Cardinal,
They that do flatter him most, say oracles
Hang at his lips: and verily I believe them:
For the devil speaks in them.
But for their sister, the right noble Duchess,
110 You never fix'd your eye on three fair medals,
Cast in one figure, of so different temper.
For her discourse, it is so full of rapture,
You only will begin, then to be sorry
When she doth end her speech: and wish, in wonder,
115 She held it less vainglory to talk much
Than your penance, to hear her: whilst she speaks,
She throws upon a man so sweet a look,
That it were able to raise one to a galliard

85 *political* cunning, scheming
103 *shrewd turns* (Q1 shewed; Q2, Q3 shrew'd; Q4 [omits])
      malicious deeds
111 *figure* form, shape; *temper* combination of elements
118 *able to raise* Q3, Q4 (Q1, Q2 able raise); *galliard* a lively
      dance

That lay in a dead palsy; and to dote
On that sweet countenance: but in that look                    120
There speaketh so divine a continence,
As cuts off all lascivious, and vain hope.
Her days are practis'd in such noble virtue,
That, sure her nights, nay more, her very sleeps,
Are more in heaven, than other ladies' shrifts.               125
Let all sweet ladies break their flatt'ring glasses,
And dress themselves in her.
*Delio.*                          Fie Antonio,
You play the wire-drawer with her commendations.
*Antonio.* I'll case the picture up: only thus much:
All her particular worth grows to this sum:                   130
She stains the time past: lights the time to come.
*Cariola.* You must attend my lady, in the gallery,
Some half an hour hence.
*Antonio.*                    I shall.
                    [*Exeunt* ANTONIO *and* DELIO.]
*Ferdinand.* Sister, I have a suit to you.
*Duchess.*                         To me, sir?
*Ferdinand.* A gentleman here: Daniel de Bosola:             135
One, that was in the galleys.
*Duchess.*                    Yes, I know him.
*Ferdinand.* A worthy fellow h'is: pray let me entreat for
The provisorship of your horse.
*Duchess.*                    Your knowledge of him
Commends him, and prefers him.
*Ferdinand.*                    Call him hither.
                         [*Exit* ATTENDANT.]
We are now upon parting. Good Lord Silvio                     140
Do us commend to all our noble friends
At the leaguer.
*Silvio.*      Sir, I shall.
*Duchess.* You are for Milan?
*Silvio.*                    I am.
*Duchess.* Bring the caroches: we'll bring you down to the
                                        haven.
[*Exeunt* DUCHESS, CARIOLA, SILVIO, CASTRUCHIO, RODERIGO,
GRISOLAN *and* JULIA.]
    *Cardinal.* Be sure you entertain that Bosola           145

125 *shrifts* confessions
128 *play the wire-drawer* spin out, over-refine
131 *stains* throws into the shade by her superiority; eclipses
140 *We are now* Q4 (Q1, Q2, Q3 We now)
142 *leaguer* Q2, Q3 (Q1 leagues; Q4 camp) a camp
143 *Duchess.* ed. (Qq. Ferd.)          144 *caroches* large coaches

For your intelligence: I would not be seen in't.
And therefore many times I have slighted him,
When he did court our furtherance: as this morning.

*Ferdinand.* Antonio, the great master of her household
Had been far fitter.

150     *Cardinal.*      You are deceiv'd in him,
His nature is too honest for such business.
He comes: I'll leave you.         [*Enter* BOSOLA]

    *Bosola.*          I was lur'd to you. [*Exit* CARDINAL.]

    *Ferdinand.* My brother here, the Cardinal, could never
Abide you.

    *Bosola.*   Never since he was in my debt.

155     *Ferdinand.* May be some oblique character in your face
Made him suspect you?

    *Bosola.*          Doth he study physiognomy?
There's no more credit to be given to th' face,
Than to a sick man's urine, which some call
The physician's whore, because she cozens him.
He did supect me wrongfully.

160     *Ferdinand.*          For that
You must give great men leave to take their times:
Distrust doth cause us seldom be deceiv'd;
You see, the oft shaking of the cedar tree
Fastens it more at root.

    *Bosola.*         Yet take heed:

165 For to suspect a friend unworthily
Instructs him the next way to suspect you,
And prompts him to deceive you.

    *Ferdinand.*        There's gold.

    *Bosola.*              So:
What follows? (Never rain'd such showers as these
Without thunderbolts i'th' tail of them;)

170 Whose throat must I cut?

    *Ferdinand.* Your inclination to shed blood rides post
Before my occasion to use you. I give you that
To live i'th' court, here: and observe the Duchess,
To note all the particulars of her haviour:

175 What suitors do solicit her for marriage
And whom she best affects: she's a young widow,
I would not have her marry again.

    *Bosola.*          No, sir?

---

146 *For your intelligence* for supplying you with secret information
166 *next* shortest, most direct        168–9 see Critical Notes.
174 *haviour* Q1 (Q2, Q3, Q4 behaviour) property, estate; behaviour

*Ferdinand.* Do not you ask the reason: but be satisfied,
I say I would not.
*Bosola.*            It seems you would create me
One of your familiars.
*Ferdinand.*        Familiar? what's that?                    180
*Bosola.* Why, a very quaint invisible devil in flesh:
An intelligencer.
*Ferdinand.*      Such a kind of thriving thing
I would wish thee: and ere long, thou mayst arrive
At a higher place by't.
*Bosola.*            Take your devils
Which hell calls angels: these curs'd gifts would make     185
You a corrupter, me an impudent traitor,
And should I take these they'll'd take me to hell.
*Ferdinand.* Sir, I'll take nothing from you that I have
                                              given.
There is a place that I procur'd for you
This morning, the provisorship o'th' horse,                190
Have you heard on't?
*Bosola.*            No.
*Ferdinand.*            'Tis yours, is't not worth thanks?
*Bosola.* I would have you curse yourself now, that your
                                              bounty,
Which makes men truly noble, e'er should make
Me a villain: oh, that to avoid ingratitude
For the good deed you have done me, I must do             195
All the ill man can invent. Thus the devil
Candies all sins o'er: and what Heaven terms vild,
That names he complemental.
*Ferdinand.*              Be yourself:
Keep your old garb of melancholy: 'twill express
You envy those that stand above your reach,               200
Yet strive not to come near 'em. This will gain
Access to private lodgings, where yourself
May, like a politic dormouse,—
*Bosola.*                  As I have seen some,
Feed in a lord's dish, half asleep, not seeming

---

185 *angels* gold coins bearing the image of St. Michael killing the
        dragon
187 *take me to hell* Q4 (Q1, Q2, Q3 take me hell)
191 *on't* Q3, Q4 (Q1 out; Q2 ont)
197 *Candies . . . o'er* ed. (Q1 Candies . . . are: Q2, Q3, Q4 Candies
        . . . ore), sugars . . . over; *vild* Q1, Q2, (Q3, Q4 vile)
198 *complemental* accomplished        203 *politic* crafty, scheming

205 To listen to any talk: and yet these rogues
Have cut his throat in a dream: what's my place?
The provisorship o'th' horse? say then my corruption
Grew out of horse dung. I am your creature.
*Ferdinand.* Away!
210 *Bosola.* Let good men, for good deeds, covet good fame,
Since place and riches oft are bribes of shame;
Sometimes the devil doth preach.        *Exit* BOSOLA.

[*Enter* CARDINAL, DUCHESS *and* CARIOLA.]

*Cardinal.* We are to part from you: and your own
                                                discretion
Must now be your director.
*Ferdinand.*        You are a widow:
215 You know already what man is: and therefore
Let not youth: high promotion, eloquence,—·
*Cardinal.* No, nor any thing without the addition, Honour,
Sway your high blood.
*Ferdinand.*        Marry? they are most luxurious,
Will wed twice.
*Cardinal.*        O fie!
*Ferdinand.*        Their livers are more spotted
Than Laban's sheep.
220 *Duchess.*        Diamonds are of most value
They say, that have pass'd through most jewellers' hands.
*Ferdinand.* Whores, by that rule, are precious.
*Duchess.*        Will you hear me?
I'll never marry—
*Cardinal.*        So most widows say:
But commonly that motion lasts no longer
225 Than the turning of an hourglass; the funeral sermon
And it, end both together.
*Ferdinand.*        Now hear me:
You live in a rank pasture here, i'th' court,
There is a kind of honey-dew that's deadly:
'Twill poison your fame; look to't; be not cunning:
230 For they whose faces do belie their hearts
Are witches, ere they arrive at twenty years,
Ay: and give the devil suck.
*Duchess.*        This is terrible good counsel.
*Ferdinand.* Hypocrisy is woven of a fine small thread,

207 *provisorship* Q2, Q3 (Q1a Prouisosr-ship, Q1b Prouisors-
        ship; Q4 [omits])
218 *luxurious* lascivious        224 *motion* impulse
230 *hearts* Q1, Q2 (Q3, Q4 heart)

Subtler than Vulcan's engine: yet, believe't,
Your darkest actions: nay, your privat'st thoughts,      235
Will come to light.
   *Cardinal.*    You may flatter yourself,
And take your own choice: privately be married
Under the eaves of night—
   *Ferdinand.*    Think't the best voyage
That e'er you made; like the irregular crab,
Which, though't goes backward, thinks that it goes right,      240
Because it goes its own way: but observe:
Such weddings may more properly be said
To be executed, than celebrated.
   *Cardinal.*         The marriage night
Is the entrance into some prison.
   *Ferdinand.*       And those joys,
Those lustful pleasures, are like heavy sleeps      245
Which do forerun man's mischief.
   *Cardinal.*       Fare you well.
Wisdom begins at the end: remember it. [*Exit* CARDINAL.]
   *Duchess.* I think this speech between you both was studied,
It came so roundly off.
   *Ferdinand.*      You are my sister,
This was my father's poniard: do you see,      250
I'll'd be loath to see't look rusty, 'cause 'twas his.
I would have you to give o'er these chargeable revels;
A visor and a mask are whispering-rooms
That were nev'r built for goodness: fare ye well:
And women like that part, which, like the lamprey,      255
Hath nev'r a bone in't.
   *Duchess.*    Fie sir!
   *Ferdinand.*    Nay,
I mean the tongue: variety of courtship;
What cannot a neat knave with a smooth tale
Make a woman believe? Farewell, lusty widow.
                  [*Exit* FERDINAND.]
   *Duchess.* Shall this move me? If all my royal kindred      260

---

234 *Vulcan's engine* the net wherein he caught his wife, Venus, with
     Mars
238 *eaves* ed. see Textual Appendix—A.
243 *executed; celebrated* are used synonymously to denote the per-
     forming of religious services. The connotations of punish-
     ment by death as opposed to rejoicing are implicit in
     Ferdinand's distinction between them.
251 *I'll'd* Q1 (Q2, Q3, Q4 I'd); *see't* Q1 (Q2, Q3, Q4 see it)
252 *to give* Q1 (Q2, Q3, Q4 give); *chargeable* expensive.
258 *neat* finely dressed; free from disease

Lay in my way unto this marriage:
I'll'd make them my low foot-steps. And even now,
Even in this hate, (as men in some great battles
By apprehending danger, have achiev'd
265  Almost impossible actions: I have heard soldiers say so,)
So I, through frights and threat'nings, will assay
This dangerous venture. Let old wives report
I winked, and chose a husband. Cariola,
To thy known secrecy I have given up
More than my life, my fame.
270       *Cariola.*          Both shall be safe:
For I'll conceal this secret from the world
As warily as those that trade in poison,
Keep poison from their children.
     *Duchess.*          Thy protestation
Is ingenious and hearty: I believe it.
Is Antonio come?
     *Cariola.*     He attends you.
275  *Duchess.*          Good dear soul,
Leave me: but place thyself behind the arras,
Where thou mayst overhear us: wish me good speed
For I am going into a wilderness,
Where I shall find nor path, nor friendly clew
To be my guide.
[CARIOLA *goes behind the arras; the* DUCHESS *draws the traverse to reveal* ANTONIO.]
280            I sent for you. Sit down:
Take pen and ink, and write. Are you ready?
     *Antonio.*                    **Yes.**
     *Duchess.* What did I say?
     *Antonio.*          That I should write somewhat.
     *Duchess.* Oh, I remember:
After these triumphs and this large expense
285  It's fit, like thrifty husbands, we inquire
What's laid up for tomorrow.
     *Antonio.* So please your beauteous excellence.


262 *I'll'd* Q1 (Q2, Q3, Q4 I'd); *foot-steps* stepping stones, rungs of
       a ladder
266 *assay* Q1, Q4 (Q2, Q3 affray)
268 *winked* closed my eyes; closed my eyes to something wrong
274 *ingenious* ingenuous
279 *nor path* Q1 (Q2, Q3, Q4 no path); *clew* thread to guide one
       through a labyrinth
284 *these triumphs* ed. see Textual Appendix—A.
285 *husbands* usual meaning; stewards

*Duchess.*                                    Beauteous?
Indeed I thank you: I look young for your sake.
You have tane my cares upon you.
    *Antonio.*                         I'll fetch your Grace
The particulars of your revenue and expense.                    290
    *Duchess.*Oh, you are an upright treasurer: but you mistook,
For when I said I meant to make inquiry
What's laid up for tomorrow: I did mean
What's laid up yonder for me.
    *Antonio.*                    Where?
    *Duchess.*                         In heaven.
I am making my will, as 'tis fit princes should          295
In perfect memory, and I pray sir, tell me
Were not one better make it smiling, thus?
Than in deep groans, and terrible ghastly looks,
As if the gifts we parted with, procur'd
That violent distraction?
    *Antonio.*          Oh, much better.          300
    *Duchess.* If I had a husband now, this care were quit:
But I intend to make you overseer;
What good deed shall we first remember? Say.
    *Antonio.* Begin with that first good deed, began i'th' world,
After man's creation, the sacrament of marriage.          305
I'ld have you first provide for a good husband,
Give him all.
    *Duchess.* All?
    *Antonio.*          Yes, your excellent self.
    *Duchess.* In a winding sheet?
    *Antonio.*                    In a couple.
    *Duchess.* St. Winifred! that were a strange will.
    *Antonio.*                              'Twere strange
If there were no will in you to marry again.          310
    *Duchess.* What do you think cf marriage?
    *Antonio.* I take't, as those that deny purgatory,
It locally contains or heaven, or hell;
There's no third place in't.
    *Duchess.*          How do you affect it?
    *Antonio.* My banishment, feeding my melancholy,          315
Would often reason thus:—

300 *distraction* Q3, Q4 (Q1, Q2 distruction)
304 *that first good deed* Q1 (Q2, Q3, Q4 that good deed that first)
306 *you first provide* Q1 (Q2, Q3, Q4 you provide)
307 *Give him* Q1, Q2 (Q3 give me; Q4 give)
308 *couple* a pair; marriage
309 *St. Winifred!* ed. (Qq. St. Winfrid)          314 *affect* like

*Duchess.*          Pray let's hear it.

*Antonio.* Say a man never marry, nor have children,
What takes that from him? only the bare name
Of being a father, or the weak delight
320   To see the little wanton ride a-cock-horse
Upon a painted stick, or hear him chatter
Like a taught starling.

*Duchess.*          Fie, fie, what's all this?
One of your eyes is bloodshot, use my ring to't,
They say 'tis very sovereign: 'twas my wedding ring,
325   And I did vow never to part with it,
But to my second husband.

*Antonio.* You have parted with it now.

*Duchess.*          Yes, to help your eyesight.

*Antonio.* You have made me stark blind.

*Duchess.*          How?

*Antonio.* There is a saucy and ambitious devil
Is dancing in this circle.

*Duchess.*          Remove him.
330   *Antonio.*          How?

*Duchess.* There needs small conjuration, when your finger
May do it: thus, is it fit?
          [*She puts the ring on his finger.*] *he kneels.*
*Antonio.*          What said you?

*Duchess.*          Sir,
This goodly roof of yours, is too low built,
I cannot stand upright in't, nor discourse,
335   Without I raise it higher: raise yourself,
Or if you please, my hand to help you: so.     [*Raises him.*

*Antonio.* Ambition, Madam, is a great man's madness,
That is not kept in chains, and close-pent rooms,
But in fair lightsome lodgings, and is girt
340   With the wild noise of prattling visitants,
Which makes it lunatic, beyond all cure.
Conceive not, I am so stupid, but I aim
Whereto your favours tend. But he's a fool
That, being a-cold, would thrust his hands i'th' fire
To warm them.
345   *Duchess.*     So, now the ground's broke,
You may discover what a wealthy mine

320 *wanton* rogue [a term of endearment]
324 *sovereign* efficacious
340 *visitants* Q3, Q4 (Q1, Q2 visitans)
342 *aim* guess, conjecture

I make you lord of.
 *Antonio.*          O my unworthiness!
 *Duchess.* You were ill to sell yourself;
This dark'ning of your worth is not like that
Which tradesmen use i'th' city; their false lights          350
Are to rid bad wares off: and I must tell you
If you will know where breathes a complete man,
(I speak it without flattery), turn your eyes,
And progress through yourself.
 *Antonio.*                    Were there nor heaven, nor hell,
I should be honest: I have long serv'd virtue,          355
And nev'r tane wages of her.
 *Duchess.*                Now she pays it.
The misery of us, that are born great,
We are forc'd to woo, because none dare woo us:
And as a tyrant doubles with his words,
And fearfully equivocates: so we          360
Are forc'd to express our violent passions
In riddles, and in dreams, and leave the path
Of simple virtue, which was never made
To seem the thing it is not. Go, go brag
You have left me heartless, mine is in your bosom,          365
I hope 'twill multiply love there. You do tremble:
Make not your heart so dead a piece of flesh
To fear, more than to love me. Sir, be confident,
What is't distracts you? This is flesh, and blood,
                                              sir,
'Tis not the figure cut in alabaster          370
Kneels at my husband's tomb. Awake, awake, man,
I do here put off all vain ceremony,
And only do appear to you, a young widow
That claims you for her husband, and like a widow,
I use but half a blush in't.
 *Antonio.*                 Truth speak for me,          375
I will remain the constant sanctuary
Of your good name.
 *Duchess.*        I thank you, gentle love,
And 'cause you shall not come to me in debt,
Being now my steward, here upon your lips

347 *lord of* Q2, Q3, Q4 (Q1 lord off.)
349 *dark'ning* obscuring
352 *will know* Q1 (Q2, Q3, Q4 would know)
358 *woo ... woo* Q3 (Q1, Q2 woe ... woe; Q4 wooe ... wooe):
        both senses are implicit in the equivocal spellings here.
359 *doubles* makes evasive movements; acts deceitfully
372 *put off* Q2, Q3, Q4 (Q1 put of)

380 I sign your *Quietus est*. This you should have begg'd now:
I have seen children oft eat sweetmeats thus,
As fearful to devour them too soon.
*Antonio*. But for your brothers?
*Duchess*.          Do not think of them:
All discord, without this circumference,
385 Is only to be pitied, and not fear'd.
Yet, should they know it, time will easily
Scatter the tempest.
*Antonio*.          These words should be mine,
And all the parts you have spoke, if some part of it
Would not have savour'd flattery.
*Duchess*.          Kneel. [*Enter* CARIOLA.]
*Antonio*.          Ha?
390 *Duchess*. Be not amaz'd, this woman's of my counsel.
I have heard lawyers say, a contract in a chamber,
*Per verba de presenti*, is absolute marriage.
Bless, Heaven, this sacred Gordian, which let violence
Never untwine.
395 *Antonio*. And may our sweet affections, like the spheres,
Be still in motion.
*Duchess*.          Quick'ning, and make
The like soft music.
*Antonio*. That we may imitate the loving palms,
Best emblem of a peaceful marriage,
400 That nev'r bore fruit divided.
*Duchess*. What can the Church force more?
*Antonio*. That Fortune may not know an accident
Either of joy or sorrow, to divide
Our fixed wishes.
*Duchess*.          How can the Church build faster?
405 We now are man and wife, and 'tis the Church
That must but echo this. Maid, stand apart,
I now am blind.

380 *Quietus est:* a *quietus* was a release or discharge and this phrase,
     in an account book, indicated that the accounts were
     correct.
384 *this circumference* see Introduction p. xix.
389 *savour'd* Q1 (Q2, Q3 favour'd; Q4 savour'd of)
392 *Per verba de presenti* ed. (Qq. *Per verba presenti*) see Critical
     Notes.
393 *Heaven* see Critical Notes on III,v, 78–79.
395 *spheres* see Critical Notes.
396 *still* always; *quick'ning* coming alive (with reference to the
     feeling of the child stirring in the womb)
401 *force* enforce, urge

*Antonio.*          What's your conceit in this?
*Duchess.* I would have you lead your fortune by the hand,
Unto your marriage bed:
(You speak in me this, for we now are one)                    410
We'll only lie, and talk together, and plot
T'appease my humorous kindred; and if you please,
Like the old tale, in *Alexander and Lodowick*,
Lay a naked sword between us, keep us chaste.
Oh, let me shroud my blushes in your bosom,                   415
Since 'tis the treasury of all my secrets.
  *Cariola.* Whether the spirit of greatness, or of woman
Reign most in her, I know not, but it shows
A fearful madness: I owe her much of pity.          *Exeunt.*


## Act II, Scene i

[*Enter* BOSOLA *and* CASTRUCHIO.]
  *Bosola.* You say you would fain be taken for an eminent
courtier?
  *Castruchio.* 'Tis the very main of my ambition.
  *Bosola.* Let me see, you have a reasonable good face for't
already, and your nightcap expresses your ears sufficient     5
largely; I would have you learn to twirl the strings of your
band with a good grace; and in a set speech, at th' end of
every sentence, to hum, three or four times, or blow your
nose, till it smart again, to recover your memory. When
you come to be a president in criminal causes, if you smile   10
upon a prisoner, hang him, but if you frown upon him, and
threaten him, let him be sure to scape the gallows.
  *Castruchio.* I would be a very merry president,—
  *Bosola.* Do not sup a nights; 'twill beget you an admirable
wit.                                                          15
  *Castruchio.* Rather it would make me have a good stomach
to quarrel, for they say your roaring boys eat meat seldom,
and that makes them so valiant: but how shall I know
whether the people take me for an eminent fellow?

412 *humorous* ill-humoured; crotchety
413 *Alexander and Lodowick* see Critical Notes.
415 *shroud* veil                          3 *main* end, purpose
5 *nightcap* white coif worn by sergeants at law; *expresses* presses
     out
6–7 *strings of your band* white tabs worn by sergeants
10 *president* presiding magistrate
17 *roaring boys* riotous bullies

20      *Bosola.* I will teach a trick to know it: give out you lie a-
dying, and if you hear the common people curse you, be
sure you are taken for one of the prime nightcaps.
[*Enter* OLD LADY]
You come from painting now?
        *Old Lady.* From what?
25      *Bosola.* Why, from your scurvy face physic: To behold
thee not painted inclines somewhat near a miracle. These
in thy face here, were deep ruts and foul sloughs, the last
progress. There was a lady in France, that having had the
smallpox, flayed the skin off her face, to make it more level;
30      and whereas before she look'd like a nutmeg grater, after
she resembled an abortive hedgehog.
        *Old Lady.* Do you call this painting?
        *Bosola.* No, no but you call it careening of an old mor-
phew'd lady, to make her disembogue again. There's rough-
35      cast phrase to your plastic.
        *Old Lady.* It seems you are well acquainted with my
closet?
        *Bosola.* One would suspect it for a shop of witchcraft,
to find in it the fat of serpents; spawn of snakes, Jews'
40      spittle, and their young children's ordure, and all these for
the face. I would sooner eat a dead pigeon, taken from the soles
of the feet of one sick of the plague, than kiss one of you
fasting. Here are two of you, whose sin of your youth is the
very patrimony of the physician, makes him renew his
45      footcloth with the spring, and change his high-priz'd
courtesan with the fall of the leaf: I do wonder you do not
loathe yourselves. Observe my meditation now:
What thing is in this outward form of man
To be belov'd? We account it ominous,
50      If nature do produce a colt, or lamb,
A fawn, or goat, in any limb resembling
A man; and fly from't as a prodigy.
Man stands amaz'd to see his deformity,
In any other creature but himself.
55      But in our own flesh, though we bear diseases

22 *nightcaps* lawyers
27 *sloughs* muddy ditches; layers of dead tissue
28 *progress* state journey    33 *careening* scraping the paint off
33–34 *morphew'd* scurfy;    34 *disembogue* come out into open sea
35 *plastic* modelling
40 *children's ordure* Q2, Q3 (Q1 children ordures; Q4 [omits])
45 *footcloth* ornamental cloth which covered the horse's back and
        hung down to the ground; it was considered a mark of
        dignity.

Which have their true names only tane from beasts,
As the most ulcerous wolf, and swinish measle;
Though we are eaten up of lice, and worms,
And though continually we bear about us
A rotten and dead body, we delight                        60
To hide it in rich tissue: all our fear,
Nay, all our terror, is lest our physician
Should put us in the ground, to be made sweet.
Your wife's gone to Rome: you two couple, and get you
To the wells at Lucca, to recover your aches.             65
            [*Exeunt* CASTRUCHIO *and* OLD LADY.]
I have other work on foot: I observe our Duchess
Is sick a-days, she pukes, her stomach seethes,
The fins of her eyelids look most teeming blue,
She wanes i'th' cheek, and waxes fat i'th' flank;
And, contrary to our Italian fashion,                     70
Wears a loose-bodied gown: there's somewhat in't.
I have a trick, may chance discover it,
A pretty one; I have bought some apricocks,
The first our spring yields.      [*Enter* ANTONIO *and* DELIO]
    *Delio.*              And so long since married?
You amaze me.
    *Antonio.*     Let me seal your lips for ever,        75
For did I think that anything but th' air
Could carry these words from you, I should wish
You had no breath at all. [*To* BOSOLA] Now sir, in your
                                        contemplation?
You are studying to become a great wise fellow?
    *Bosola.* Oh sir, the opinion of wisdom is a foul tetter, 80
that runs all over a man's body: if simplicity direct us to
have no evil, it directs us to a happy being. For the subtlest
folly proceeds from the subtlest wisdom. Let me be simply
honest.
    *Antonio.* I do understand your inside.               85
    *Bosola.* Do you so?
    *Antonio.* Because you would not seem to appear to th'
                                        world
Puff'd up with your preferment, you continue
This out of fashion melancholy; leave it, leave it.

57 *ulcerous wolf:* lupus = ulcer; *swinish measle:* measle(s), applied
     to a skin disease in swine, was confused with ordinary measles.
65 *Lucca* see III, ii, 313 note.
67 *seethes* is inwardly agitated
68 *fins* rims, edges; *teeming* pregnant
73 *apricocks* apricots
80 *tetter* Q4 (Q1, tettor; Q2, Q3 terror) skin eruption

90   *Bosola.* Give me leave to be honest in any phrase, in any
compliment whatsoever: shall I confess myself to you? I
look no higher than I can reach: they are the gods, that
must ride on winged horses, a lawyer's mule of a slow pace
will both suit my disposition and business. For, mark me,
95   when a man's mind rides faster than his horse can gallop
they quickly both tire.
   *Antonio.* You would look up to Heaven, but I think
The devil, that rules i'th' air, stands in your light.
   *Bosola.* Oh, sir, you are lord of the ascendant, chief man
100  with the Duchess: a duke was your cousin-german,
remov'd. Say you were lineally descended from King
Pippin, or he himself, what of this? Search the heads of the
greatest rivers in the world, you shall find them but bubbles
of water. Some would think the souls of princes were
105  brought forth by some more weighty cause, than those of
meaner persons; they are deceiv'd, there's the same hand to
them: the like passions sway them; the same reason, that
makes a vicar go to law for a tithe-pig, and undo his neighbours, makes them spoil a whole province, and batter down
110  goodly cities with the cannon.

[*Enter* DUCHESS, OLD LADY, LADIES.]

   *Duchess.* Your arm Antonio, do I not grow fat?
I am exceeding short-winded. Bosola,
I would have you, sir, provide for me a litter,
Such a one, as the Duchess of Florence rode in.
   *Bosola.* The duchess us'd one, when she was great with
115                                         child.
   *Duchess.* I think she did. Come hither, mend my ruff,
Here; when? thou art such a tedious lady; and
Thy breath smells of lemon peels; would thou hadst done;
Shall I sound under thy fingers? I am
So troubled with the mother.
120  *Bosola* [*aside*].          I fear too much.
   *Duchess.* I have heard you say that the French courtiers

99 *lord of the ascendant* (in astronomy), the ruling planet, dominat-
     ing influence
100 *cousin-german* first cousin
101–102 *King Pippin* see Critical Notes.
108 *go to* Q1 (Q2, Q3, Q4 to go to)
117 *when?* an exclamation of impatience
118 *lemon peels* ed. see Textual Appendix—A.
119 *sound* Q1 (Q2, Q3, Q4 swound) swoon
120 *mother* hysterical passion characterized by a sense of swelling
     and suffocation; *too* Q2, Q3, Q4 (Q1 to)
121 *courtiers* Q2, Q3, Q4 (Q1 courties)

Wear their hats on 'fore the king.
*Antonio.*                    I have seen it.
*Duchess.* In the presence?
*Antonio.*                    Yes:
*Duchess.* Why should not we bring up that fashion?
'Tis ceremony more than duty, that consists                    125
In the removing of a piece of felt:
Be you the example to the rest o'th' court,
Put on your hat first.
*Antonio.*          You must pardon me:
I have seen, in colder countries than in France,
Nobles stand bare to th' prince; and the distinction          130
Methought show'd reverently.
*Bosola.* I have a present for your Grace.
*Duchess.*                    For me sir?
*Bosola.* Apricocks, Madam.
*Duchess.*              O sir, where are they?
I have heard of none to-year.
*Bosola [aside].*          Good, her colour rises.
*Duchess.* Indeed I thank you: they are wondrous fair
                              ones.  135
What an unskilful fellow is our gardener!
We shall have none this month.
*Bosola.* Will not your Grace pare them?
*Duchess:* No, they taste of musk, methinks; indeed they
                              do.
*Bosola.* I know not: yet I wish your Grace had par'd
                              'em.  140
*Duchess.* Why?
*Bosola.*     I forgot to tell you the knave gard'ner,
Only to raise his profit by them the sooner,
Did ripen them in horse-dung.
*Duchess.*              Oh you jest.
[*to* ANTONIO] You shall judge: pray taste one.
*Antonio.*                    Indeed Madam,  145
I do not love the fruit.
*Duchess.*          Sir, you are loth
To rob us of our dainties: 'tis a delicate fruit,
They say they are restorative?

122 *'fore* ed. (Q1, Q2 fore; Q3, Q4 before)
124 speech–prefix: Q4 *Duch.* (Q1, Q2, Q3 continue as Antonio's
          speech)
130 *bare* bare-headed
131 *Methought* Q4 (Q1, Q2, Q3 My thought)
134 *to-year* Q1, Q2, Q3 (Q4 this year), *cf.* to-day

*Bosola.*                    'Tis a pretty art,
This grafting.
*Duchess.*    'Tis so: a bett'ring of nature.
150    *Bosola.* To make a pippin grow upon a crab,
A damson on a black-thorn: [*aside*] How greedily she eats
                                                    them!
A whirlwind strike off these bawd farthingales,
For, but for that, and the loose-bodied gown,
I should have discover'd apparently
155    The young springal cutting a caper in her belly.
*Duchess.* I thank you, Bosola: they were right good ones,
If they do not make me sick.
*Antonio.*                How now Madam?
*Duchess.* This green fruit: and my stomach are not friends.
How they swell me!
160    *Bosola* [*aside*]. Nay, you are too much swell'd already.
*Duchess.* Oh, I am in an extreme cold sweat.
*Bosola.*                    I am very sorry.    [*Exit*]
*Duchess.* Lights to my chamber! O, good Antonio,
I fear I am undone.

                                        *Exit* DUCHESS.

*Delio.*        Lights there, lights!
*Antonio.* O my most trusty Delio, we are lost:
165    I fear she's fall'n in labour: and there's left
No time for her remove.
*Delio.*                Have you prepar'd
Those ladies to attend her? and procur'd
That politic safe conveyance for the midwife
Your duchess plotted?
*Antonio.*            I have.
170    *Delio.* Make use then of this forc'd occasion:
Give out that Bosola hath poison'd her,
With these apricocks: that will give some colour
For her keeping close.
*Antonio.*        Fie, fie, the physicians
Will then flock to her.
*Delio.*            For that you may pretend

---

149 *This grafting:* a double entendre
150 *a pippin* Q1 (Q2, Q3 pippin; Q4 Pippins); *a crab* crab-apple
        tree
152 *farthingales* hooped petticoats
154 *apparently* manifestly, openly        155 *springal* stripling
164 *most trusty* Q1 (Q2, Q3 trusty; Q4 O my Dear Friend)
168 *politic* cunning            173 *close* shut up from observation

She'll use some prepar'd antidote of her own,                    175
Lest the physicians should repoison her.
*Antonio.* I am lost in amazement: I know not what to
think on't.
                                                    *Ex[eunt].*

## Scene ii

[*Enter* BOSOLA *and* OLD LADY]

*Bosola.* So, so: there's no question but her tetchiness and
most vulturous eating of the apricocks, are apparent signs
of breeding, now?
*Old Lady.* I am in haste, sir.
*Bosola.* There was a young waiting-woman, had a        5
monstrous desire to see the glass-house—
*Old Lady.* Nay, pray let me go:
*Bosola.* And it was only to know what strange instrument
it was, should swell up a glass to the fashion of a woman's
belly.                                                            10
*Old Lady.* I will hear no more of the glass-house, you are
still abusing women!
*Bosola.* Who, I? no, only, by the way now and then,
mention your frailties. The orange tree bears ripe and
green fruit and blossoms altogether. And some of you give    15
entertainment for pure love: but more, for more precious
reward. The lusty spring smells well: but drooping autumn
tastes well. If we have the same golden showers, that rained
in the time of Jupiter the Thunderer: you have the same
Danaes still, to hold up their laps to receive them: didst    20
thou never study the mathematics?
*Old Lady.* What's that, sir?
*Bosola.* Why, to know the trick how to make a many lines
meet in one centre. Go, go; give your foster-daughters good
counsel: tell them, that the devil takes delight to hang at a  25
woman's girdle, like a false rusty watch, that she cannot
discern how the time passes.
[*Exit* OLD LADY; *enter* ANTONIO, DELIO, RODERIGO, GRISOLAN.]
*Antonio.* Shut up the court gates.
*Roderigo.*                Why sir? what's the danger?

1 *tetchiness* irritability (Q1 teatchiues [i.e. turned *n*]; Q2, Q3
       teatchives; Q4 substitutes 'eager')
2 *apparent* obvious          6 *glass-house* glass factory
14 *bears* Q3, Q4 (Q1, Q2 beare)
20 *Danaes* ed. (Q1, Q2 *Danes;* Q3 *Dames;* Q4 *Danae's*); see Critical
       Notes.

*Antonio.* Shut up the posterns presently: and call
All the officers o'th' court.

30      *Grisolan.*               I shall instantly.          [*Exit.*
*Antonio.* Who keeps the key o'th' park-gate?
*Roderigo.*                                      Forobosco.
*Antonio.* Let him bring't presently.       [*Exit* RODERIGO.

[*Enter* SERVANTS, GRISOLAN, RODERIGO.]

*1 Servant.* Oh, gentlemen o'th' court, the foulest treason!
*Bosola* [*aside*]. If that these apricocks should be poison'd,
                                                          now;
Without my knowledge!

35      *1 Servant.*            There was taken even now
A Switzer in the Duchess' bedchamber.
*2 Servant.*                            A Switzer?
*1 Servant.* With a pistol in his great cod-piece.
*Bosola.*                                    Ha, ha, ha.
*1 Servant.* The cod-piece was the case for't.
*2 Servant.*               There was a cunning traitor.
Who would have search'd his cod-piece?

40      *1 Servant.* True, if he had kept out of the ladies' chambers:
And all the moulds of his buttons were leaden bullets.
*2 Servant.* Oh wicked cannibal: a fire-lock in's cod-piece?
*1 Servant.* 'Twas a French plot upon my life.
*2 Servant.*               To see what the devil can do.
*Antonio.* All the officers here?
*Servants.*                  We are.
*Antonio.*                            Gentlemen,

45  We have lost much plate you know; and but this evening
Jewels, to the value of four thousand ducats
Are missing in the Duchess' cabinet.
Are the gates shut?
      *1 Servant.*   Yes.
         *Antonio.*            'Tis the Duchess' pleasure
Each officer be lock'd into his chamber

50  Till the sun-rising; and to send the keys
Of all their chests, and of their outward doors
Into her bedchamber. She is very sick.
*Roderigo.* At her pleasure.
*Antonio.* She entreats you take't not ill. The innocent

29, 32 *presently* immediately
37 *cod-piece* an appendage, often ornamented, to the close-fitting
         hose or breeches of 15th–17th centuries
42 *cannibal* bloodthirsty savage    44 *officers* Q2, Q3, Q4 (Q1 offices)
47 *cabinet* private apartment, boudoir
54 *take't* Q1 (Q2, Q3 tak't; Q4 ta'kt)

Shall be the more approv'd by it.                                         55
   *Bosola.* Gentleman o'th' wood-yard, where's your Switzer
                                                  now?
   *1 Servant.* By this hand 'twas credibly reported by one
o'th' black-guard.
            [*Exeunt* BOSOLA, RODERIGO *and* SERVANTS.]
   *Delio.* How fares it with the Duchess?
   *Antonio.*                              She's expos'd
Unto the worst of torture, pain, and fear.                               60
   *Delio.* Speak to her all happy comfort.
   *Antonio.* How I do play the fool with mine own danger!
You are this night, dear friend, to post to Rome,
My life lies in your service.
   *Delio.*                    Do not doubt me.
   *Antonio.* Oh, 'tis far from me: and yet fear presents me        65
Somewhat that looks like danger.
   *Delio.*                          Believe it,
'Tis but the shadow of your fear, no more:
How superstitiously we mind our evils!
The throwing down salt, or crossing of a hare;
Bleeding at nose, the stumbling of a horse:                              70
Or singing of a cricket, are of power
To daunt whole man in us. Sir, fare you well:
I wish you all the joys of a bless'd father;
And, for my faith, lay this unto your breast,
Old friends, like old swords, still are trusted best.                    75
                                 [*Exit* DELIO.]

[*Enter* CARIOLA *with a child.*]

   *Cariola.* Sir, you are the happy father of a son,
Your wife commends him to you.
   *Antonio.*                          Blessed comfort!
For heaven' sake tend her well: I'll presently
Go set a figure for's nativity.
                                 *Exeunt.*

55 *approv'd* established as good, commended
56 *wood-yard* a yard where wood is stored, or chopped, especially
    for fuel
58 *th'black-guard* the meanest drudges; scullions and turnspits
66 *looks* Q2, Q3, Q4 (Q1 looke)
74 *unto* (Q2, Q3, into; Q4 [omits])
75 S.D. supplied by Q4.
79 *figure* horoscope

## Scene iii

[*Enter* BOSOLA *with a dark lanthorn.*]

*Bosola.* Sure I did hear a woman shriek: list, ha?
And the sound came, if I receiv'd it right,
From the Duchess' lodgings: there's some stratagem
In the confining all our courtiers
5   To their several wards. I must have part of it,
My intelligence will freeze else. List again,
It may be 'twas the melancholy bird,
Best friend of silence, and of solitariness,
The owl, that scream'd so: ha! Antonio?

[*Enter* ANTONIO *with a candle, his sword drawn.*]

*Antonio.* I heard some noise: who's there? What art
10                                         thou? Speak.
*Bosola.* Antonio! Put not your face nor body
To such a forc'd expression of fear,
I am Bosola; your friend.
*Antonio.*                Bosola!
[*aside*] This mole does undermine me—heard you not
A noise even now?
*Bosola.*          From whence?
15   *Antonio.*                        From the Duchess' lodging.
*Bosola.* Not I: did you?
*Antonio.*                I did: or else I dream'd.
*Bosola.* Let's walk towards it.
*Antonio.*                        No. It may be 'twas
But the rising of the wind.
*Bosola.*                   Very likely.
Methinks 'tis very cold, and yet you sweat.
You look wildly.
20   *Antonio.*      I have been setting a figure
For the Duchess' jewels.
*Bosola.*                Ah: and how falls your question?
Do you find it radical?
*Antonio.*              What's that to you?
'Tis rather to be question'd what design,

S.D.s are supplied from Q4.                5 *wards* apartments
   6 *intelligence* conveying secret information
10 *who's* Q3, Q4 (Q1, Q2 whose)
22 *radical* fit to be judged

When all men were commanded to their lodgings,
Makes you a night-walker.
    *Bosola.*           In sooth I'll tell you:      25
Now all the court's asleep, I thought the devil
Had least to do here; I come to say my prayers,
And if it do offend you, I do so,
You are a fine courtier.
    *Antonio [aside].*    This fellow will undo me.
You gave the Duchess apricocks to-day,      30
Pray heaven they were not poison'd!
    *Bosola.* Poison'd! a Spanish fig
For the imputation.
    *Antonio.*        Traitors are ever confident,
Till they are discover'd. There were jewels stol'n too,
In my conceit, none are to be suspected
More than yourself.
    *Bosola.*        You are a false steward.      35
    *Antonio.* Saucy slave! I'll pull thee up by the roots.
    *Bosola.* May be the ruin will crush you to pieces.
    *Antonio.* You are an impudent snake indeed, sir,
Are you scarce warm, and do you show your sting?
    *Bosola.* . . .
    *Antonio.* You libel well, sir.
    *Bosola.*         No sir, copy it out:      40
And I will set my hand to't.
    *Antonio.*        My nose bleeds.
One that were superstitious, would count
This ominous: when it merely comes by chance.
Two letters, that are wrought here for my name
Are drown'd in blood!      45
Mere accident: for you, sir, I'll take order:
I'th' morn you shall be safe: [*aside*] 'tis that must colour
Her lying-in: sir, this door you pass not:
I do not hold it fit, that you come near
The Duchess' lodgings, till you have quit yourself;      50
[*aside*] *The great are like the base; nay, they are the same,*
*When they seek shameful ways to avoid shame.*
                                    *Ex[it.]*

31 *a Spanish fig:* a contemptuous term, accompanied by an in-
      decent gesture
34 *conceit* opinion
39–40: line(s) omitted—see Textual Appendix—A.
40 speech–prefix: Q1 *Ant.;* Q2, Q3, Q4 continue previous speech
      without further prefix.
44 *wrought* Q1, Q2 (Q3, Q4 wrote) embroidered (in a handker-
      chief)

*Bosola.* Antonio here about did drop a paper,
Some of your help, false friend: oh, here it is.
55   What's here? a child's nativity calculated?
[*reads:*] *The Duchess was deliver'd of a son, 'tween the hours*
*twelve and one, in the night: Anno Dom: 1504.* (*that's this*
*year*) *decimo nono Decembris,* (*that's this night*) *taken*
*according to the Meridian of Malfi* (*that's our Duchess: happy*
60   *discovery*). *The Lord of the first house, being combust in the*
*ascendant, signifies short life: and* Mars *being in a human*
*sign, join'd to the tail of the Dragon, in the eight house, doth*
*threaten a violent death;* Cætera non scrutantur.
Why now 'tis most apparent. This precise fellow
65   Is the Duchess' bawd: I have it to my wish.
This is a parcel of intelligency
Our courtiers were cas'd up for! It needs must follow,
That I must be committed, on pretence
Of poisoning her: which I'll endure, and laugh at.
70   If one could find the father now: but that
Time will discover. Old Castruchio
I'th' morning posts to Rome; by him I'll send
A letter, that shall make her brothers' galls
O'erflow their livers. This was a thifty way.
75   *Though lust do masque in ne'er so strange disguise*
*She's oft found witty, but is never wise.*          [*Exit.*]

## Scene iv

[*Enter* CARDINAL *and* JULIA.]

*Cardinal.* Sit: thou art my best of wishes; prithee tell me
What trick didst thou invent to come to Rome,
Without thy husband?
    *Julia.*          Why, my Lord, I told him
I came to visit an old anchorite
Here, for devotion.
5      *Cardinal.*          Thou art a witty false one:
I mean to him.
      *Julia.*          You have prevailed with me

54 *false friend* i.e. the dark lanthorn
56–63 see Critical Notes.
63 *Cætera non scrutantur* Q2, Q3, Q4 (Q1 Cæteta non scrutantur)
    'the rest is not examined'
67 *cas'd* Q2, Q3, Q4 (Q1 caside)
75 *masque* take part in a masque; *ne'er* ed. (Q1, Q2 *nea'r*; Q3, Q4
    *ne're*)
5 *Here* Q2, Q3, Q4 (Q1 Heare)

Beyond my strongest thoughts: I would not now
Find you inconstant.
*Cardinal*            Do not put thyself
To such a voluntary torture, which proceeds
Out of your own guilt.
   *Julia.*            How, my Lord?
   *Cardinal.*                      You fear          10
My constancy, because you have approv'd
Those giddy and wild turnings in yourself.
   *Julia.* Did you e'er find them?
   *Cardinal.*                Sooth, generally for women;
A man might strive to make glass malleable,
Ere he should make them fixed.
   *Julia.*            So, my Lord.          15
   *Cardinal.* We had need go borrow that fantastic glass
Invented by Galileo the Florentine,
To view another spacious world i'th' moon,
And look to find a constant woman there.
   *Julia.* This is very well, my Lord.
   *Cardinal.*                Why do you weep?          20
Are tears your justification? The selfsame tears
Will fall into your husband's bosom, lady,
With a loud protestation that you love him
Above the world. Come, I'll love you wisely,
That's jealously, since I am very certain          25
You cannot me make cuckold.
   *Julia.*                I'll go home
To my husband.
   *Cardinal.*      You may thank me, lady,
I have taken you off your melancholy perch,
Bore you upon my fist, and show'd you game,
And let you fly at it. I pray thee kiss me.          30
When thou wast with thy husband, thou wast watch'd
Like a tame elephant: (still you are to thank me.)
Thou hadst only kisses from him, and high feeding,
But what delight was that? 'Twas just like one
That hath a little fing'ring on the lute,          35
Yet cannot tune it: (still you are to thank me.)
   *Julia.* You told me of a piteous wound i'th' heart,

12 *turnings* Q3, Q4 (Q1, Q2 turning)
16–19 see Critical Notes.
25 *That's jealously* Q1, Q4 (Q2, Q3 That jealously)
26 *me make* Q1 (Q2, Q4 make me; Q3 make me a)
28–30: the Cardinal speaks as if Julia were a falcon.
30 *I pray thee* ed. (Q1 I pray the; Q2, Q3 I prethee; Q4 I prithee)

**R—C**

And a sick liver, when you wooed me first,
And spake like one in physic.
    *Cardinal.*           Who's that?
                          *[Enter* SERVANT.]
40    Rest firm, for my affection to thee,
Lightning moves slow to't.
    *Servant.*         Madam, a gentleman
That's come post from Malfi, desires to see you.
    *Cardinal.* Let him enter, I'll withdraw.    *Exit.*
    *Servant.*             He says
Your husband, old Castruchio, is come to Rome,
45    Most pitifully tir'd with riding post.
             *[Exit* SERVANT; *enter* DELIO.]
    *Julia.* Signior Delio! *[aside]* 'tis one of my old suitors.
    *Delio.* I was bold to come and see you.
    *Julia.*           Sir, you are welcome.
    *Delio.* Do you lie here?
    *Julia.*          Sure, your own experience
Will satisfy you no; our Roman prelates
Do not keep lodging for ladies.
50    *Delio.*         Very well.
I have brought you no commendations from your husband,
For I know none by him.
    *Julia.*      I hear he's come to Rome?
    *Delio.* I never knew man and beast, of a horse and a knight,
55    So weary of each other; if he had had a good back,
He would have undertook to have borne his horse,
His breach was so pitifully sore.
    *Julia.*       Your laughter
Is my pity.
    *Delio.*   Lady, I know not whether
You want money, but I have brought you some.
    *Julia.* From my husband?
    *Delio.*        No, from mine own allowance.
60    *Julia.* I must hear the condition, ere I be bound to take it.
    *Delio.* Look on't, 'tis gold, hath it not a fine colour?
    *Julia.* I have a bird more beautiful.
    *Delio.*       Try the sound on't.
    *Julia.* A lute-string far exceeds it;

39 *one in physic* someone under medical surveillance
41 *to't* in comparison to it
47 *to come and* Q1 (Q2, Q3 *and come to*; Q4 [changes line completely]); *you are* Q2, Q3 (Q1 your are, Q4 you're)
49 *no* Q1, Q4 (Q2, Q3 now)
59 *mine own* Q1, Q2 (Q3, Q4 my own)

It hath no smell, like cassia or civet,
Nor is it physical, though some fond doctors                    65
Persuade us, seethe't in cullises. I'll tell you,
This is a creature bred by—                    [Enter SERVANT]
    Servant.                    Your husband's come,
Hath deliver'd a letter to the Duke of Calabria,
That, to my thinking, hath put him out of his wits.
                                        [Exit SERVANT.]
    Julia. Sir, you hear,                                        70
Pray let me know your business and your suit,
As briefly as can be.
    Delio.                    With good speed. I would wish you,
At such time, as you are non-resident
With your husband, my mistress.
    Julia. Sir, I'll go ask my husband if I shall,              75
And straight return your answer.                    Exit.
    Delio.                    Very fine,
Is this her wit, or honesty that speaks thus?
I heard one say the Duke was highly mov'd
With a letter sent from Malfi. I do fear
Antonio is betray'd: how fearfully                              80
Shows his ambition now; unfortunate Fortune!
*They pass through whirlpools, and deep woes do shun,*
*Who the event weigh, ere the action's done.*          Exit.

### Scene v

[*Enter*] CARDINAL, *and* FERDINAND, *with a letter.*

*Ferdinand.* I have this night dig'd up a mandrake.
    *Cardinal.*                    Say you?
*Ferdinand.* And I am grown mad with't.
    *Cardinal.*                    What's the prodigy?
*Ferdinand.* Read there, a sister damn'd, she's loose, i'th'
                                        hilts:

64 *cassia* coarser kind of cinnamon; *civet* perfume with a strong
    musky smell
65 *physical* medicinal
66 *seethe't* ed. (Q1, Q2 seeth's; Q3 seeth'd; Q4 Persuade us, 'tis a
    Cordial.); *cullises* strengthening broths, made by bruising
    meat
77 *honesty* honour in the sense of chastity; *speaks* Q1 (Q2, Q3,
    Q4 speak)
S.D. Q1, Q2, Q3 (Q4 *Cardinal and Ferdinand, Furious, with a
    Letter*)
1 *mandrake* see Critical Notes; *Say you?* What do you say?
2 *prodigy* ed. (Q1, Q2 progedy; Q3, Q4 prodegy)
3 *damn'd* Q2, Q3, Q4 (Q1 dampn'd), *loose i'th' hilts* unreliable
    (here in the sense of unchaste)

Grown a notorious strumpet.

*Cardinal.*                              Speak lower.

*Ferdinand.*                                        Lower?

5   Rogues do not whisper't now, but seek to publish't,
As servants do the bounty of their lords,
Aloud; and with a covetous searching eye,
To mark who note them. Oh confusion seize her,
She hath had most cunning bawds to serve her turn,

10  And more secure conveyances for lust,
Than towns of garrison, for service.

*Cardinal.*                              Is't possible?
Can this be certain?

*Ferdinand.*                    Rhubarb, oh for rhubarb
To purge this choler; here's the cursed day
To prompt my memory, and here't shall stick

15  Till of her bleeding heart I make a sponge
To wipe it out.

*Cardinal.*          Why do you make yourself
So wild a tempest?

*Ferdinand.*              Would I could be one,
That I might toss her palace 'bout her ears,
Root up her goodly forests, blast her meads,

20  And lay her general territory as waste,
As she hath done her honour's.

*Cardinal.*                              Shall our blood?
The royal blood of Aragon and Castile,
Be thus attainted?

*Ferdinand.*              Apply desperate physic,
We must not now use balsamum, but fire,

25  The smarting cupping-glass, for that's the mean
To purge infected blood, such blood as hers.
There is a kind of pity in mine eye,
I'll give it to my handkercher; and now 'tis here,
I'll bequeath this to her bastard.

*Cardinal.*                              What to do?

*Ferdinand.* Why, to make soft lint for his mother's

30                                                    wounds,

10 *secure conveyances* safe passages
11 *service* military service; sexual intercourse
12–13 see Critical Notes.
14 *here't* Q2, Q3, Q4 (Q1 here'it)
21 *honour's* ed. see Textual Appendix—A.
24 *balsamum* aromatic healing ointment
28 *handkercher* Q1, Q2 (Q3, Q4 handkerchief)
30 *mother's wounds* Q4 (Q1 mother wounds; Q2, Q3 mothers
        wounds)

When I have hewed her to pieces.
*Cardinal.*                    Curs'd creature!
Unequal nature, to place women's hearts
So far upon the left side.
*Ferdinand.*              Foolish men,
That e'er will trust their honour in a bark,
Made of so slight, weak bulrush, as is woman,                    35
Apt every minute to sink it!
*Cardinal.* Thus ignorance, when it hath purchas'd honour,
It cannot wield it.
*Ferdinand.*          Methinks I see her laughing,
Excellent hyena! Talk to me somewhat, quickly,
Or my imagination will carry me                    40
To see her in the shameful act of sin.
*Cardinal.* With whom?
*Ferdinand.* Happily, with some strong thigh'd bargeman;
Or one o'th' wood-yard, that can quoit the sledge
Or toss the bar, or else some lovely squire                    45
That carries coals up to her privy lodgings.
*Cardinal.* You fly beyond your reason.
*Ferdinand.*                         Go to, mistress!
'Tis not your whore's milk, that shall quench my wild-fire
But your whore's blood.
*Cardinal.* How idly shows this rage! which carries you,                    50
As men convey'd by witches, through the air
On violent whirlwinds: this intemperate noise
Fitly resembles deaf men's shrill discourse,
Who talk aloud, thinking all other men
To have their imperfection.
*Ferdinand.*              Have not you                    55
My palsy?
*Cardinal.* Yes, I can be angry
Without this rupture; there is not in nature
A thing, that makes man so deform'd, so beastly
As doth intemperate anger; chide yourself:
You have divers men, who never yet express'd                    60
Their strong desire of rest but by unrest,

32 *unequal* unjust, partial          33 *left side* see Critical Notes.
35 *is woman* Q1 (Q2, Q3, Q4 this woman)
37 *purchas'd* obtained          43 *Happily* haply, maybe
44 *quoit the sledge* throw the sledge-hammer
46 *privy* Q1 (Q2, Q3 private; Q4 [omits])
47 *Go to, mistress!* an expression of disapprobation; also, go to it!
48 *shall* Q1 (Q2, Q3, Q4 can); *wild-fire* furious and destructive fire,
          easily ignited and difficult to extinguish; eruptive skin
          disease in children

By vexing of themselves. Come, put yourself
In tune.
    *Ferdinand.* So, I will only study to seem
The thing I am not. I could kill her now,
In you, or in myself, for I do think
It is some sin in us, Heaven doth revenge
By her.
    *Cardinal.* Are you stark mad?
    *Ferdinand.*                   I would have their bodies
Burnt in a coal-pit, with the ventage stopp'd,
That their curs'd smoke might not ascend to Heaven:
Or dip the sheets they lie in, in pitch or sulphur,
Wrap them in't, and then light them like a match:
Or else to boil their bastard to a cullis,
And give't his lecherous father, to renew
The sin of his back.
    *Cardinal.*      I'll leave you.
    *Ferdinand.*               Nay, I have done;
I am confident, had I been damn'd in hell,
And should have heard of this, it would have put me
Into a cold sweat. In, in, I'll go sleep:
Till I know who leaps my sister, I'll not stir:
That known, I'll find scorpions to string my whips,
And fix her in a general eclipse.       *Exeunt.*

### Act III, Scene i

[*Enter* ANTONIO *and* DELIO]

    *Antonio.* Our noble friend, my most beloved Delio,
Oh, you have been a stranger long at court,
Came you along with the Lord Ferdinand?
    *Delio.* I did, sir, and how fares your noble Duchess?
    *Antonio.* Right fortunately well. She's an excellent
Feeder of pedigrees: since you last saw her,
She hath had two children more, a son and daughter.
    *Delio.* Methinks 'twas yesterday. Let me but wink,
And not behold your face, which to mine eye
Is somewhat leaner: verily I should dream
It were within this half hour.
    *Antonio.* You have not been in law, friend Delio,

66 see Critical Notes on III,v, 79–80.
72 *cullis* see II, iv, 66 note.    73 *give't* Q1 (Q2, Q3, Q4 giv't)
79 *string* Q1 (Q2, Q3, Q4 sting)  80 *general eclipse* total eclipse
8 *wink* to close the eyes

Nor in prison, nor a suitor at the court,
Nor begg'd the reversion of some great man's place,
Nor troubled with an old wife, which doth make          15
Your time so insensibly hasten.
   *Delio.*              Pray sir tell me,
Hath not this news arriv'd yet to the ear
Of the Lord Cardinal?
   *Antonio.*         I fear it hath;
The Lord Ferdinand, that's newly come to court,
Doth bear himself right dangerously.
   *Delio.*              Pray why?          20
   *Antonio.* He is so quiet, that he seems to sleep
The tempest out, as dormice do in winter;
Those houses, that are haunted, are most still,
Till the devil be up.
   *Delio.*         What say the common people?
   *Antonio.* The common rabble do directly say          25
She is a strumpet.
   *Delio.*        And your graver heads,
Which would be politic, what censure they?
   *Antonio.* They do observe I grow to infinite purchase
The left-hand way, and all suppose the Duchess
Would amend it, if she could. For, say they,          30
Great princes, though they grudge their officers
Should have such large and unconfined means
To get wealth under them, will not complain
Lest thereby they should make them odious
Unto the people: for other obligation          35
Of love, or marriage, between her and me,
They never dream of.
[*Enter* FERDINAND, DUCHESS *and* BOSOLA.]
   *Delio.*        The Lord Ferdinand
Is going to bed.
   *Ferdinand.*  I'll instantly to bed,
For I am weary: I am to bespeak
A husband for you.
   *Duchess.*     For me, sir! pray who is't?          40
   *Ferdinand.* The great Count Malateste.
   *Duchess.*         Fie upon him,
A count? He's a mere stick of sugar-candy,

16 *insensibly* Q3 (Q1 inseucibly; Q2 insencibly; Q4 [omits])
27 *censure* to form an opinion
28 *purchase* substance, acquired wealth   29 *left-hand* sinister
37 *dream of* Q3, Q4 (Q1 dream off; Q2 dreame of)
39 *to bespeak* ed. (Q1 to be be-speake; Q2 to be-speake; Q3 Q4
     to be-speak)

You may look quite thorough him: when I choose
A husband, I will marry for your honour.
 *Ferdinand.* You shall do well in't. How is't, worthy
45               Antonio?
 *Duchess.* But, sir, I am to have private conference with
              you,
About a scandalous report is spread
Touching mine honour.
  *Ferdinand.*  Let me be ever deaf to't:
One of Pasquil's paper bullets, court calumny,
50 A pestilent air, which princes' palaces
Are seldom purg'd of. Yet, say that it were true,
I pour it in your bosom, my fix'd love
Would strongly excuse, extenuate, nay deny
Faults were they apparent in you. Go, be safe
In your own innocency.
55 *Duchess.*    Oh bless'd comfort,
This deadly air is purg'd.
     *Exeunt* [DUCHESS, ANTONIO, DELIO.]
 *Ferdinand.*    Her guilt treads on
Hot burning cultures. Now Bosola,
How thrives our intelligence?
 *Bosola.*    Sir, uncertainly:
'Tis rumour'd she hath had three bastards, but
By whom, we may go read i'th' stars.
60 *Ferdinand.*    Why some
Hold opinion, all things are written there.
 *Bosola.* Yes, if we could find spectacles to read them;
I do suspect, there hath been some sorcery
Us'd on the Duchess.
 *Ferdinand.*  Sorcery, to what purpose?
65 *Bosola.* To make her dote on some desertless fellow,
She shames to acknowledge.
 *Ferdinand.*  Can your faith give way
To think there's power in potions, or in charms,
To make us love, whether we will or no?
 *Bosola.* Most certainly.
70 *Ferdinand.* Away, these are mere gulleries, horrid things

43 *thorough* Q1, Q2 (Q3, Q4 through)
48 *mine* Q1, Q2 (Q3, Q4 my)
49 *Pasquil's paper bullets* pasquinades (satirical verses originally
  produced for amusement)
51 *purg'd of* ed. (Q1, Q2, Q3 purg'd off; Q4 [omits]).
54 *were* Q3 (Q1, Q2 where; Q4 [omits])
57 *cultures* coulters, plough-shares

Invented by some cheating mountebanks
To abuse us. Do you think that herbs, or charms
Can force the will? Some trials have been made
In the foolish practice; but the ingredients
Were lenative poisons, such as are of force            75
To make the patient mad; and straight the witch
Swears, by equivocation, they are in love.
The witchcraft lies in her rank blood: this night
I will force confession from her. You told me
You had got, within these two days, a false key       80
Into her bed-chamber.
    *Bosola.*        I have.
    *Ferdinand.*           As I would wish.
    *Bosola.* What do you intend to do?
    *Ferdinand.*           Can you guess?
    *Bosola.*                   No.
    *Ferdinand.* Do not ask then.
He that can compass me, and know my drifts,
May say he hath put a girdle 'bout the world,          85
And sounded all her quick-sands.
    *Bosola.*           I do not
Think so.
    *Ferdinand.* What do you think then, pray?
    *Bosola.*               That you
Are your own chronicle too much: and grossly
Flatter yourself.
    *Ferdinand.*   Give me thy hand; I thank thee.
I never gave pension but to flatterers,                90
Till I entertained thee: farewell,
*That friend a great man's ruin strongly checks,*
*Who rails into his belief all his defects.*        *Exeunt.*


### Scene ii

[*Enter* DUCHESS, ANTONIO *and* CARIOLA]

    *Duchess.* Bring me the casket hither, and the glass;
You get no lodging here to-night, my lord.
    *Antonio.* Indeed, I must persuade one.
    *Duchess.*             Very good:
I hope in time 'twill grow into a custom,

75 *lenative poisons* ? violent aphrodisiacs (Lucas)
78 *blood* Q2, Q3, Q4 (Q1 bood)
82 *guess* Q3, Q4 (Q1, Q2 ghesse)

5   That noblemen shall come with cap and knee,
To purchase a night's lodging of their wives.
*Antonio.* I must lie here.
*Duchess.*                    Must? you are a lord of mis-rule.
*Antonio.* Indeed, my rule is only in the night.
*Duchess.* To what use will you put me?
*Antonio.*                          We'll sleep together.
10  *Duchess.* Alas, what pleasure can two lovers find in sleep?
*Cariola.* My lord, I lie with her often: and I know
She'll much diquiet you.
*Antonio.*                    See, you are complain'd of.
*Cariola.* For she's the sprawling'st bedfellow.
*Antonio.* I shall like her the better for that.
15  *Cariola.* Sir, shall I ask you a question?
*Antonio.* I pray thee Cariola.
*Cariola.* Wherefore still, when you lie with my lady
Do you rise so early?
*Antonio.*                    Labouring men,
Count the clock oft'nest Cariola,
Are glad when their task's ended.
20  *Duchess.*                    I'll stop your mouth [*kisses him*].
*Antonio.* Nay, that's but one, Venus had two soft doves
To draw her chariot: I must have another [*kisses her*].
When wilt thou marry, Cariola?
*Cariola.*                    Never, my lord.
*Antonio.* O fie upon this single life: forgo it.
25  We read how Daphne, for her peevish flight
Became a fruitless bay-tree; Sirinx turn'd
To the pale empty reed; Anaxarete
Was frozen into marble: whereas those
Which married, or prov'd kind unto their friends
30  Were, by a gracious influence, transhap'd
Into the olive, pomegranate, mulberry:
Became flowers, precious stones, or eminent stars.
*Cariola.* This is vain poetry: but I pray you tell me,
If there were propos'd me wisdom, riches, and beauty,
35  In three several young men, which should I choose?
*Antonio.* 'Tis a hard question. This was Paris' case
And he was blind in't, and there was great cause:

5 *with cap and knee* with cap in hand and bended knee; humbly
7 *lord of mis-rule* master of the revels (which took place at night);
    lord of the rule of misses (mistresses)
25–28 see Critical Notes.
25 *peevish* perverse; *flight* ed. (Qq slight)
26 *Sirinx* Q4 (Q1a Sirina; Q1b, Q2, Q3 Siriux)
27 *Anaxarete* ed. (Q1a Anaxorate: Q1b, Q2, Q3, Q4 Anaxarate)

For how was't possible he could judge right,
Having three amorous goddesses in view,
And they stark naked? 'Twas a motion                40
Were able to benight the apprehension
Of the severest counsellor of Europe.
Now I look on both your faces, so well form'd
It puts me in mind of a question, I would ask.
    *Cariola*. What is't?
    *Antonio*.        I do wonder why hard favour'd ladies    45
For the most part, keep worse-favour'd waiting-women,
To attend them, and cannot endure fair ones.
    *Duchess*. Oh, that's soon answer'd.
Did you ever in your life know an ill painter
Desire to have his dwelling next door to the shop        50
Of an excellent picture-maker? 'Twould disgrace
His face-making, and undo him. I prithee
When were we so merry? My hair tangles.
    *Antonio* [*aside to* CARIOLA]. Pray thee, Cariola, let's steal
                                   forth the room,
And let her talk to herself: I have divers times        55
Serv'd her the like, when she hath chaf'd extremely.
I love to see her angry: softly Cariola.
                    *Exeunt* [ANTONIO *and* CARIOLA.]
    *Duchess*. Doth not the colour of my hair 'gin to change?
When I wax grey, I shall have all the court
Powder their hair with arras, to be like me:            60
You have cause to love me, I ent'red you into my heart.

    [*Enter* FERDINAND, *unseen*.]

Before you would vouchsafe to call for the keys.
We shall one day have my brothers take you napping.
Methinks his presence, being now in court,
Should make you keep your own bed: but you'll say        65
Love mix'd with fear is sweetest. I'll assure you
You shall get no more children till my brothers

38 *could* Q1 (Q2, Q3, Q4 should)        40 *motion* display
41 *apprehension* Q2, Q3 (Q1a approbation; Q1b apprehention;
    Q4 [omits])
46 *waiting* Q3, Q4 (Q1a wai-ting; Q1b waieting; Q2 wayting)
50 *his dwelling* Q1b, Q2, Q3, Q4 (Q1a the dwelling).
53 *so merry* Q1 (Q2, Q3, Q4 merry)
56 *hath* Q1 (Q2, Q3 had; Q4 has)
60 *arras* the white powder of orris-root, smelling of violets
61 *I enter'd you into* Q1 (Q2, Q3 I enter'd into; Q4 it enter'd
    into)

Consent to be your gossips. Have you lost your tongue?
[*She sees* FERDINAND *holding a poniard.*]
'Tis welcome:
70  For know, whether I am doom'd to live, or die,
I can do both like a prince.
                    FERDINAND *gives her a poniard.*
    *Ferdinand.*            Die then, quickly.
Virtue, where art thou hid? What hideous thing
Is it, that doth eclipse thee?
    *Duchess.*              Pray sir hear me—
    *Ferdinand.* Or is it true, thou art but a bare name,
And no essential thing?
    *Duchess.*        Sir—
75  *Ferdinand.*            Do not speak.
    *Duchess.* No sir:
I will plant my soul in mine ears, to hear you.
    *Ferdinand.* Oh most imperfect light of human reason,
That mak'st us so unhappy, to foresee
80  What we can least prevent. Pursue thy wishes:
And glory in them: there's in shame no comfort,
But to be past all bounds and sense of shame.
    *Duchess.* I pray sir, hear me: I am married—
    *Ferdinand.*                            So.
    *Duchess.* Happily, not to your liking: but for that
85  Alas: your shears do come untimely now
To clip the bird's wings, that's already flown.
Will you see my husband?
    *Ferdinand.*              Yes, if I could change
Eyes with a basilisk.
    *Duchess.*            Sure, you came hither
By his confederacy.
    *Ferdinand.*        The howling of a wolf
90  Is music to thee, screech-owl; prithee peace.
Whate'er thou art, that hast enjoy'd my sister,
(For I am sure thou hear'st me), for thine own sake

68 *your gossips* godparents of your children
73 *eclipse* Q4 (Q1 ecclipze; Q2, Q3 clip)
78 *most* Q1 (Q2, Q3, Q4 must)
79 *mak'st us* Q4 (Q1, Q2, Q3 mak'st)
84 *Happily* Q1, Q2, Q3 (Q4 Happly) maybe, perhaps
88 *basilisk:* both breath and sight of this fabulous creature had
        power to kill.
89 *confederacy* Q3, Q4 (Q1, Q2 consideracy)
90 *thee* Q4 (Q1, Q2, Q3 the)
92 *hear'st* Q4 (Q1 hearst; Q2, Q3 heardst); *thine* Q1, Q4 (Q2,
        Q3 mine)

Let me not know thee. I came hither prepar'd
To work thy discovery: yet am now persuaded
It would beget such violent effects                    95
As would damn us both. I would not for ten millions
I had beheld thee; therefore use all means
I never may have knowledge of thy name;
Enjoy thy lust still, and a wretched life,
On that condition. And for thee, vild woman,           100
If thou do wish thy lecher may grow old
In thy embracements, I would have thee build
Such a room for him, as our anchorites
To holier use inhabit. Let not the sun
Shine on him, till he's dead. Let dogs and monkeys     105
Only converse with him, and such dumb things
To whom nature denies use to sound his name.
Do not keep a paraquito, lest she learn it;
If thou do love him, cut out thine own tongue
Lest it bewray him.
  *Duchess.*  Why might not I marry?        110
I have not gone about, in this, to create
Any new world, or custom.
  *Ferdinand.*  Thou art undone:
And thou hast tane that massy sheet of lead
That hid thy husband's bones, and folded it
About my heart.
  *Duchess.*  Mine bleeds for't.
  *Ferdinand.*  Thine? thy heart?        115
What should I name't, unless a hollow bullet
Fill'd with unquenchable wild-fire?
  *Duchess.*  You are in this
Too strict: and were you not my princely brother
I would say too wilful. My reputation
Is safe.
  *Ferdinand.* Dost thou know what reputation is?   120
I'll tell thee, to small purpose, since th'instruction
Comes now too late:
Upon a time Reputation, Love and Death
Would travel o'er the world: and it was concluded
That they should part, and take three several ways.    125

95 *such* Q1 (Q2, Q3, Q4 so)
96 *damn* Q3, Q4 (Q1 dampe; Q2 damne)
100 *vild* (Q1 vilde) vile (Q2 wilde; Q3 wild; Q4 vile)
107 *use to sound* ability to sound
110 *bewray* Q1, Q2, Q3 (Q4 betray)
116 *hollow bullet* cannon ball  117 *wild-fire* cf. II, v, 48 note.

Death told them, they should find him in great battles:
Or cities plagu'd with plagues. Love gives them counsel
To inquire for him 'mongst unambitious shepherds,
Where dowries were not talk'd of: and sometimes
130    'Mongst quiet kindred, that had nothing left
By their dead parents. 'Stay', quoth Reputation,
'Do not forsake me: for it is my nature
If once I part from any man I meet
I am never found again.' And so, for you:
135    You have shook hands with Reputation,
And made him invisible. So fare you well.
I will never see you more.
    *Duchess.*             Why should only I,
Of all the other princes of the world
Be cas'd up, like a holy relic? I have youth,
And a little beauty.
140        *Ferdinand.*       So you have some virgins,
That are witches. I will never see thee more.    *Exit.*

    *Enter* [CARIOLA *and*] ANTONIO *with a pistol.*

    *Duchess.* You saw this apparition?
    *Antonio.*                Yes: we are
Betray'd; how came he hither? I should turn
This, to thee, for that. [*points the pistol at* CARIOLA.]
    *Cariola.*         Pray sir do: and when
145    That you have cleft my heart, you shall read there,
Mine innocence.
    *Duchess.*       That gallery gave him entrance.
    *Antonio.* I would this terrible thing would come again,
That, standing on my guard, I might relate
My warrantable love. Ha! what means this?
    *Duchess.* He left this with me.   *she shows the poniard.*
150        *Antonio.*            And it seems, did wish
You would use it on yourself?
    *Duchess.*         His action seem'd
To intend so much.
    *Antonio.*       This hath a handle to't,
As well as a point: turn it towards him, and
So fasten the keen edge in his rank gall. [*knocking*]
How now? Who knocks? More earthquakes?
155        *Duchess.*                I stand
As if a mine, beneath my feet, were ready
To be blown up.
    *Cariola.*      'Tis Bosola.
    *Duchess.*          Away!

Oh misery, methinks unjust actions
Should wear these masks and curtains; and not we.
You must instantly part hence: I have fashion'd it already.     160

                  *Ex[it]* ANT[ONIO; *enter* BOSOLA.]

  *Bosola.* The Duke your brother is tane up in a whirlwind;
Hath took horse, and's rid post to Rome.
  *Duchess.*                       So late?
  *Bosola.* He told me, as he mounted into th' saddle,
You were undone.
  *Duchess.*        Indeed, I am very near it.
  *Bosola.* What's the matter?     165
  *Duchess.* Antonio, the master of our household
Hath dealt so falsely with me, in's accounts:
My brother stood engag'd with me for money
Tane up of certain Neapolitan Jews,
And Antonio lets the bonds be forfeit.     170
  *Bosola.* Strange: [*aside*] this is cunning.
  *Duchess.*                   And hereupon
My brother's bills at Naples are protested
Against. Call up our officers.
  *Bosola.*              I shall.               *Exit.*

[*Enter* ANTONIO]

  *Duchess.* The place that you must fly to, is Ancona,
Hire a house there. I'll send after you     175
My treasure, and my jewels: our weak safety
Runs upon enginous wheels: short syllables
Must stand for periods. I must now accuse you
Of such a feigned crime, as Tasso calls
*Magnanima mensogna:* a noble lie,     180
'Cause it must shield our honours: hark, they are coming.

[*Enter* BOSOLA *and* OFFICERS.]

  *Antonio.* Will your Grace hear me?
  *Duchess.* I have got well by you: you have yielded me
A million of loss; I am like to inherit
The people's curses for your stewardship.     185
You had the trick, in audit time to be sick,
Till I had sign'd your *Quietus*; and that cur'd you

---

167 *in's* in his                170 *lets* Q4 (Q1, Q2, Q3 let's)
173 *our* Q1 (Q2, Q3, Q4 the)
177 *enginous* ed. (Q1 engeneous; Q2, Q3, Q4 ingenious) i.e. those
        of a clock where small and almost imperceptible move-
        ment produces obvious motion of the hands.
180 *Magnanima mensogna* see Critical Notes.

Without help of a doctor. Gentlemen,
I would have this man be an example to you all:
190 So shall you hold my favour. I pray let him;
For h'as done that, alas! you would not think of,
And, because I intend to be rid of him,
I mean not to publish. Use your fortune elsewhere.
    *Antonio.* I am strongly arm'd to brook my overthrow,
195 As commonly men bear with a hard year:
I will not blame the cause on't; but do think
The necessity of my malevolent star
Procures this, not her humour. O the inconstant
And rotten ground of service, you may see;
200 'Tis ev'n like him that, in a winter night,
Takes a long slumber, o'er a dying fire
As loth to part from't: yet parts thence as cold,
As when he first sat down.
    *Duchess.*          We do confiscate,
Towards the satisfying of your accounts,
All that you have.
205     *Antonio.*      I am all yours; and 'tis very fit
All mine should be so.
    *Duchess.*        So, sir; you have your pass.
    *Antonio.* You may see, gentlemen, what 'tis to serve
A prince with body and soul.          *Exit.*
    *Bosola.* Here's an example for extortion; what moisture is
210 drawn out of the sea, when foul weather comes, pours down,
and runs into the sea again.
    *Duchess.* I would know what are your opinions
Of this Antonio.
    *2 Officer.* He could not abide to see a pig's head gaping,
215 I thought your Grace would find him a Jew:
    *3 Officer.* I would you had been his officer, for your own
sake.
    *4 Officer.* You would have had more money.
    *1 Officer.* He stopp'd his ears with black wool: and to
220 those came to him for money said he was thick of hearing.
    *2 Officer.* Some said he was an hermaphrodite, for he
could not abide a woman.
    *4 Officer.* How scurvy proud he would look, when the

190 *let him* let him go, leave him alone
191 *h'as* he has
209 *extortion* Q1, Q2 (Q3, Q4 exhortation)
216 *his officer* Q1 (Q2, Q3, Q4 officer)
219 *hermaphrodite* ed. (Q1, Q3, Q4 hermophrodite; Q2 hermophro-
    bite)
223 *he would* Q1 (Q2, Q3, Q4 would he)

treasury was full. Well, let him go.

*1 Officer.* Yes, and the chippings of the butt'ry fly after     225
him, to scour his gold chain.

*Duchess.* Leave us. What do you think of these?

                                      *Exeunt* [OFFICERS].

*Bosola.* That these are rogues, that in's prosperity,
But to have waited on his fortune, could have wish'd
His dirty stirrup riveted through their noses:     230
And follow'd after's mule, like a bear in a ring.
Would have prostituted their daughters to his lust;
Made their first born intelligencers; thought none happy
But such as were born under his bless'd planet;
And wore his livery: and do these lice drop off now?     235
Well, never look to have the like again;
He hath left a sort of flatt'ring rogues behind him,
Their doom must follow. Princes pay flatterers,
In their own money. Flatterers dissemble their vices,
And they dissemble their lies, that's justice.     240
Alas, poor gentleman,—

*Duchess.* Poor! he hath amply fill'd his coffers.

*Bosola.* Sure he was too honest. Pluto the god of riches,
When he's sent, by Jupiter, to any man
He goes limping, to signify that wealth     245
That comes on God's name, comes slowly; but when he's
                                        sent
On the devil's errand, he rides post, and comes in by
                                      scuttles.
Let me show you what a most unvalu'd jewel
You have, in a wanton humour, thrown away.
To bless the man shall find him. He was an excellent     250
Courtier, and most faithful; a soldier, that thought it
As beastly to know his own value too little,
As devilish to acknowledge it too much;
Both his virtue and form deserv'd a far better fortune:
His discourse rather delighted to judge itself, than show
                                        itself.     255

225 *chippings* parings of a crust of bread
226 *gold chain* Q1, Q4 (Q2, Q3 golden chain), the steward's badge
    of office
229 *his fortune* Q1, Q4 (Q2, Q3 this fortune)
231 *in a ring* with a ring through his nose
234 *bless'd planet* Q1 (Q2, Q3, Q4 planet)
237 *a sort* a collection                243 *Pluto* see Critical Notes.
247 *On* Q2, Q3, Q4 (Q1 One); *by scuttles* scuttling
248 *unvalu'd* invaluable
255 *discourse* conversational power

His breast was fill'd with all perfection,
And yet it seem'd a private whisp'ring room:
It made so little noise of't.
*Duchess.*                    But he was basely descended.
*Bosola.* Will you make yourself a mercenary herald,
260 Rather to examine men's pedigrees, than virtues?
You shall want him:
For know an honest statesman to a prince,
Is like a cedar, planted by a spring,
The spring bathes the tree's root, the grateful tree
265 Rewards it with his shadow: you have not done so;
I would sooner swim to the Bermoothas on
Two politicians' rotten bladders, tied
Together with an intelligencer's heart string
Than depend on so changeable a prince's favour.
270 Fare thee well, Antonio, since the malice of the world
Would needs down with thee, it cannot be said yet
That any ill happened unto thee,
Considering thy fall was accomplished with virtue.
*Duchess.* Oh, you render me excellent music.
*Bosola.*                              Say you?
275 *Duchess.* This good one that you speak of, is my husband.
*Bosola.* Do I not dream? Can this ambitious age
Have so much goodness in't, as to prefer
A man merely for worth: without these shadows
Of wealth, and painted honours? possible?
*Duchess.* I have had three children by him.
280 *Bosola.*                              Fortunate lady,
For you have made your private nuptial bed
The humble and fair seminary of peace.
No question but many an unbenefic'd scholar
Shall pray for you, for this deed, and rejoice
285 That some preferment in the world can yet
Arise from merit. The virgins of your land,
That have no dowries, shall hope your example
Will raise them to rich husbands. Should you want
Soldiers, 'twould make the very Turks and Moors
290 Turn Christians, and serve you for this act.
Last, the neglected poets of your time,
In honour of this trophy of a man,

266 *Bermoothas* ed. Bermudas (Q1a, Q1b Bermoothes; Q1c, Q2,
    Q3, Bermootha's; Q4 [omits]); see Critical Notes.
267 *politicians* crafty and intriguing schemers
278: Q1 (Q2, Q3, Q4 [omit])
282 *seminary* nursery; seed bed

Rais'd by that curious engine, your white hand,
Shall thank you in your grave for't; and make that
More reverend than all the cabinets                                  295
Of living princes. For Antonio,
His fame shall likewise flow from many a pen,
When heralds shall want coats, to sell to men.
    *Duchess.* As I taste comfort, in this friendly speech,
So would I find concealment—
    *Bosola.*                              Oh the secret of my prince,   300
Which I will wear on th'inside of my heart.
    *Duchess.* You shall take charge of all my coin, and jewels,
And follow him, for he retires himself
To Ancona.
    *Bosola.* So.
    *Duchess.* Whither, within few days,
I mean to follow thee.
    *Bosola.*                      Let me think:                        305
I would wish your Grace to feign a pilgrimage
To Our Lady of Loretto, scarce seven leagues
From fair Ancona, so may you depart
Your country with more honour, and your flight
Will seem a princely progress, retaining                             310
Your usual train about you.
    *Duchess.*                          Sir, your direction
Shall lead me, by the hand.
    *Cariola.*                        In my opinion,
She were better progress to the baths at Lucca,
Or go visit the Spa
In Germany: for, if you will believe me,                            315
I do not like this jesting with religion,
This feigned pilgrimage.
    *Duchess.*                        Thou art a superstitious fool:
Prepare us instantly for our departure.
Past sorrows, let us moderately lament them,
For those to come, seek wisely to prevent them.                     320
                              *Exit* [DUCHESS *with* CARIOLA].
    *Bosola.* A politician is the devil's quilted anvil,
He fashions all sins on him, and the blows
Are never heard; he may work in a lady's chamber,
As here for proof. What rests, but I reveal
All to my lord? Oh, this base quality                               325

298 *coats* coats of arms
313 *Lucca* 13 miles N.E. of Pisa; cf. II,i, 65.
314 *Spa* was in Belgium but, to the Elizabethans, all the Low
        Countries were alike considered 'Dutch' or 'German'.

Of intelligencer! Why, every quality i'th' world
Prefers but gain, or commendation:
Now for this act, I am certain to be rais'd,
*And men that paint weeds, to the life, are prais'd.*          *Exit.*


### Scene iii

[*Enter*] CARDINAL, FERDINAND, MALATESTE, PESCARA, SILVIO,
DELIO.

    *Cardinal.* Must we turn soldier then?
    *Malateste.*                                 The Emperor,
Hearing your worth that way, ere you attain'd
This reverend garment, joins you in commission
With the right fortunate soldier, the Marquis of Pescara
And the famous Lannoy.
5    *Cardinal.*                     He that had the honour
Of taking the French king prisoner?
    *Malateste.*                                The same.
Here's a plot drawn for a new fortification
At Naples.
    *Ferdinand.* This great Count Malateste, I perceive
Hath got employment.
    *Delio.*                       No employment, my lord,
10  A marginal note in the muster book, that he is
A voluntary lord.
    *Ferdinand.* He's no soldier?
    *Delio.* He has worn gunpowder, in's hollow tooth,
For the tooth-ache.
    *Silvio.* He comes to the leaguer with a full intent
15  To eat fresh beef, and garlic; means to stay
Till the scent be gone, and straight return to court.
    *Delio.* He hath read all the late service,
As the City chronicle relates it,
And keeps two painters going, only to express
Battles in model.

1 *The Emperor* Charles V
4 *Marquis of Pescara* Ferdinando Franceso d'Avolos (1489–1525)
5 *Lannoy* Charles de Lannoy, Viceroy of Naples (*c.* 1487–1527)
      to whom alone Francis I of France would surrender his
      sword at Pavia in 1525. The reference to the event here is
      obviously anachronistic.
7 *plot* diagram                              17 *service* military operations
19 *keeps* Q2, Q3 (Q1 keepe; Q4 [omits]); *painters* Q1c (Q1a,
    Q1b pewterers)

*Silvio.*                    Then he'll fight by the book.          20
*Delio.* By the almanac, I think,
To choose good days, and shun the critical.
That's his mistress' scarf.
*Silvio.*                    Yes, he protests
He would do much for that taffeta,—
*Delio.* I think he would run away from a battle          25
To save it from taking prisoner.
*Silvio.*                    He is horribly afraid
Gunpowder will spoil the perfume on't,—
*Delio.* I saw a Dutchman break his pate once
For calling him pot-gun; he made his head
Have a bore in't, like a musket.          30
*Silvio.* I would he had made a touch-hole to't.
He is indeed a guarded sumpter-cloth
Only for the remove of the court.          [*Enter* BOSOLA.]
*Pescara.* Bosola arriv'd? What should be the business?
Some falling out amongst the cardinals.          35
These factions amongst great men, they are like
Foxes, when their heads are divided:
They carry fire in their tails, and all the country
About them goes to wrack for't.
*Silvio.*                    What's that Bosola?
*Delio.* I knew him in Padua, a fantastical scholar, like          40
such who study to know how many knots was in Hercules'
club; of what colour Achilles' beard was, or whether Hector
were not troubled with the toothache. He hath studied
himself half blear-ey'd, to know the true symmetry of
Caesar's nose by a shoeing-horn: and this he did to gain the          45
name of a speculative man.
*Pescara.* Mark Prince Ferdinand,
A very salamander lives in's eye,
To mock the eager violence of fire.
*Silvio.* That cardinal hath made more bad faces with his          50
oppression than ever Michael Angelo made good ones: he
lifts up's nose, like a foul porpoise before a storm,—
*Pescara.* The Lord Ferdinand laughs.
*Delio.* Like a deadly cannon, that lightens ere it smokes.

---

20 *he'll* Q2, Q3 (Q1 hel; Q4 [omits])
23 *critical* related to the crisis or turning point; determining the
        issue
32 *guarded sumpter-cloth* decorated saddle cloth used on such
        special occasions as a royal progress
39 *goes to wrack* is devastated (cf. 'goes to wrack and ruin')
43 *hath* Q1, Q2 (Q3, Q4 had)

55      *Pescara.* These are your true pangs of death,
The pangs of life, that struggle with great statesmen,—
     *Delio.* In such a deformed silence, witches whisper their
charms.
     *Cardinal.* Doth she make religion her riding hood
To keep her from the sun and tempest?
60      *Ferdinand.*                That:
That damns her. Methinks her fault and beauty
Blended together, show like leprosy,
The whiter, the fouler. I make it a question
Whether her beggarly brats were ever christ'ned.
65      *Cardinal.* I will instantly solicit the state of Ancona
To have them banish'd.
     *Ferdinand.*         You are for Loretto?
I shall not be at your ceremony; fare you well:
Write to the Duke of Malfi, my young nephew
She had by her first husband, and acquaint him
With's mother's honesty.
     *Bosola.*          I will.
70      *Ferdinand.*         Antonio!
A slave, that only smell'd of ink and counters,
And nev'r in's life look'd like a gentleman,
But in the audit time: go, go presently,
Draw me out an hundred and fifty of our horse,
75      And meet me at the fort-bridge.            *Exeunt.*


### Scene iv

[*Enter*] TWO PILGRIMS *to the Shrine of Our Lady of
Loretto.*

     *1 Pilgrim.* I have not seen a goodlier shrine than this,
Yet I have visited many.
     *2 Pilgrim.*            The Cardinal of Aragon
Is this day to resign his cardinal's hat;
His sister duchess likewise is arriv'd
5      To pay her vow of pilgrimage. I expect

62 *like leprosy* Q1, Q2 (Q3, Q4 like a leprosy)
65 *state* rulers (collective)
69 *her first* Q1, Q3 (Q2 first; Q4 [omits])
71 *counters* small discs used for calculating in accountancy
72 *life* Q2, Q3, Q4 (Q1 like)
74 *hundred* Q2, Q3, Q4 (Q1 hundreth)
Scene iv [omitted entirely by Q4] 1 *shrine* Q1, Q3 (Q2 shrive)

A noble ceremony.

    *1 Pilgrim.*    No question.—They come.

*Here the ceremony of the Cardinal's instalment in the habit
of a soldier: perform'd in delivering up his cross, hat, robes,
and ring at the shrine; and investing him with sword, helmet,
shield, and spurs. Then* ANTONIO, *the* DUCHESS *and their
children, having presented themselves at the shrine, are (by a
form of banishment in dumb-show expressed towards them by
the* CARDINAL, *and the state of* ANCONA) *banished. During
all which ceremony this ditty is sung to very solemn music,
by divers churchmen; and then*

                                        *Exeunt.*

> *Arms and honours deck thy story,*
> *To thy fame's eternal glory,*
> *Adverse fortune ever fly thee,*    The Au-
> *No disastrous fate come nigh thee.*  thor dis-    10
>                                    claims
> *I alone will sing thy praises,*    this Ditty
> *Whom to honour virtue raises;*   to be his
> *And thy study that divine is,*
> *Bent to martial discipline is:*
> *Lay aside all those robes lie by thee,*    15
> *Crown thy arts with arms: they'll beautify thee.*
>
> *O worthy of worthiest name, adorn'd in this manner,*
> *Lead bravely thy forces on, under war's warlike banner:*
> *O mayst thou prove fortunate in all martial courses,*
> *Guide thou still by skill, in arts and forces:*    20

*Victory attend thee nigh, whilst fame sings loud thy powers,*
*Triumphant conquest crown thy head, and blessings pour down*
                                 *showers.*

    *1 Pilgrim.* Here's a strange turn of state: who would have
                                     thought
So great a lady would have match'd herself
Unto so mean a person? Yet the Cardinal    25
Bears himself much too cruel.

    *2 Pilgrim.*           They are banish'd.

    *1 Pilgrim.* But I would ask what power hath this state
Of Ancona, to determine of a free prince?

S.D.: *habit* Q1b (Q1a *order*); *of a soldier* Q2, Q3 (Q1 *a soldier*);
    *shrine* Q1 (Q2 *shrive*; Q3 *shrieve*); *banishment in dumb-show
    expressed* Q1b (Q1a *banishment expressed*)
Q1a has title 'The Hymne', omitted in Q1b, and side note reads
    Hymn for Ditty. The authorship of the ditty is unknown.
26 *much too cruel* Q1 (Q2, Q3 *too cruel*)
28 *determine of* come to a judicial decision about

*2 Pilgrim.* They are a free state sir, and her brother show'd
30  How that the Pope, forehearing of her looseness,
Hath seiz'd into th' protection of the Church
The dukedom which she held as dowager.
   *1 Pilgrim.* But by what justice?
   *2 Pilgrim.*                    Sure I think by none,
Only her brother's instigation.
35   *1 Pilgrim.* What was it, with such violence he took
Off from her finger?
   *2 Pilgrim.*          'Twas her wedding-ring,
Which he vow'd shortly he would sacrifice
To his revenge.
   *1 Pilgrim.*   Alas Antonio!
If that a man be thrust into a well,
40  No matter who sets hand to't, his own weight
Will bring him sooner to th' bottom. Come, let's hence
Fortune makes this conclusion general,
*All things do help th'unhappy man to fall.*          *Exeunt.*


## Scene v

[*Enter*] ANTONIO, DUCHESS, CHILDREN, CARIOLA, SERVANTS.

*Duchess.* Banish'd Ancona?
   *Antonio.*                    Yes, you see what power
Lightens in great men's breath.
   *Duchess.*                    Is all our train
Shrunk to this poor remainder?
   *Antonio.*                    These poor men,
Which have got little in your service, vow
5  To take your fortune. But your wiser buntings
Now they are fledg'd are gone.
   *Duchess.*                    They have done wisely;
This puts me in mind of death: physicians thus,
With their hands full of money, use to give o'er

29 *free state:* At this time Ancona was a semi-independent republic
     under papal protection; *sir, and* Q1b (Q1a *and*)
31 *Hath* Q1b (Q1a *Had*)
34 *brother's* ed. (Qq *brothers*) i.e. the Cardinal's instigation (cf. III,
     iii, 65–6), but *brothers'* is a possible reading.
36 *off* Q2, Q3 (Q1 *of*)
1 *Banish'd Ancona?* Qq., Sampson (Dyce, Lucas: Banish'd
     Ancona!)
3 *These poor* Q1 (Q2, Q3, Q4 These are poor)
5 *buntings* small birds related to the lark family

Their patients.

*Antonio.*     Right the fashion of the world:
From decay'd fortunes every flatterer shrinks,          10
Men cease to build where the foundation sinks.
*Duchess.* I had a very strange dream tonight.
*Antonio.*                              What was't?
*Duchess.* Methought I wore my coronet of state,
And on a sudden all the diamonds
Were chang'd to pearls.
*Antonio.*               My interpretation          15
Is, you'll weep shortly; for to me, the pearls
Do signify your tears.
*Duchess.*               The birds, that live i'th' field
On the wild benefit of nature, live
Happier than we; for they may choose their mates,
And carol their sweet pleasures to the spring.          20

[*Enter* BOSOLA *with a letter which he presents to the* DUCHESS.]

*Bosola.* You are happily o'ertane.
*Duchess.*                          From my brother?
*Bosola.* Yes, from the Lord Ferdinand; your brother,
All love, and safety—
*Duchess.*               Thou dost blanch mischief;
Wouldst make it white. See, see; like to calm weather
At sea before a tempest, false hearts speak fair          25
To those they intend most mischief. [*She reads*] *A Letter:
Send* Antonio *to me; I want his head in a business.*
(A politic equivocation)
He doth not want your counsel, but your head;
That is, he cannot sleep till you be dead.          30
And here's another pitfall, that's strew'd o'er
With roses: mark it, 'tis a cunning one:
*I stand engaged for your husband for several debts at Naples:
let not that trouble him, I had rather have his heart than his
money.*          35
And I believe so too.
*Bosola.*           What do you believe?
*Duchess.* That he so much distrusts my husband's love,
He will by no means believe his heart is with him
Until he see it. The devil is not cunning enough

---

9 *Right* just     12 *What was't?* Q1, Q4 (Q2, Q3 What is't?)
18 *benefit* deed of kindness; favour; gift
24 *like to calm weather* Q1, Q4 (Q2, Q3 like to the calm weather)
28 *politic equivocation* cunning use of words of double meaning
with intent to deceive

40    To circumvent us in riddles.
          *Bosola.* Will you reject that noble and free league
      Of amity and love which I present you?
          *Duchess.* Their league is like that of some politic kings
      Only to make themselves of strength and power
45    To be our after-ruin: tell them so.
          *Bosola.* And what from you?
          *Antonio.*                    Thus tell them: I will not come.
          *Bosola.* And what of this?
          *Antonio.*                    My brothers have dispers'd
      Bloodhounds abroad; which till I hear are muzzl'd
      No truce, though hatch'd with ne'er such politic skill
50    Is safe, that hangs upon our enemies' will.
      I'll not come at them.
          *Bosola.*              This proclaims your breeding.
      Every small thing draws a base mind to fear;
      As the adamant draws iron: fare you well sir,
      You shall shortly hear from's.                    *Exit.*
          *Duchess.*              I suspect some ambush:
55    Therefore by all my love; I do conjure you
      To take your eldest son, and fly towards Milan;
      Let us not venture all this poor remainder
      In one unlucky bottom.
          *Antonio.*              You counsel safely.
      Best of my life, farewell. Since we must part
60    Heaven hath a hand in't: but no otherwise
      Than as some curious artist takes in sunder
      A clock, or watch, when it is out of frame
      To bring't in better order.
          *Duchess.*              I know not which is best,
      To see you dead, or part with you. Farewell boy,
65    Thou art happy, that thou hast not understanding
      To know thy misery. For all our wit
      And reading brings us to a truer sense
      Of sorrow. In the eternal Church, sir,
      I do hope we shall not part thus.
          *Antonio.*              O be of comfort,
70    Make patience a noble fortitude:
      And think not how unkindly we are us'd.
      *Man, like to cassia, is prov'd best being bruis'd.*
          *Duchess.* Must I like to a slave-born Russian,

47 *brothers* i.e. brothers-in-law          53 *adamant* loadstone
58 *bottom* (hold of a) ship
68 *eternal Church* the Church triumphant
73 *Russian* Q1 (Q2, Q3, Q4 Ruffian)

Account it praise to suffer tyranny?
And yet, O Heaven, thy heavy hand is in't.                   75
I have seen my little boy oft scourge his top,
And compar'd myself to't: nought made me e'er go right,
But Heaven's scourge-stick.
        *Antonio.*              Do not weep:
Heaven fashion'd us of nothing; and we strive
To bring ourselves to nothing. Farewell Cariola,          80
And thy sweet armful. [*To the* DUCHESS] If I do never see
                                              thee more,
Be a good mother to your little ones,
And save them from the tiger: fare you well.
    *Duchess:* Let me look upon you once more: for that speech
Came from a dying father: your kiss is colder               85
Than I have seen an holy anchorite
Give to a dead man's skull.
    *Antonio.* My heart is turn'd to a heavy lump of lead,
With which I sound my danger: fare you well.
                            *Exit [with elder* SON.]
    *Duchess.* My laurel is all withered.                      90
    *Cariola.* Look, Madam, what a troop of armed men
Make toward us.

        *Enter* BOSOLA *with a guard [vizarded].*

    *Duchess.*       O, they are very welcome:
When Fortune's wheel is over-charg'd with princes,
The weight makes it move swift. I would have my ruin
Be sudden. I am your adventure, am I not?                   95
    *Bosola.* You are: you must see your husband no more,—
    *Duchess.* What devil art thou, that counterfeits Heaven's
                                              thunder?
    *Bosola.* Is that terrible? I would have you tell me whether
Is that note worse that frights the silly birds
Out of the corn; or that which doth allure them            100
To the nets? You have heark'ned to the last too much.
    *Duchess.* O misery! like to a rusty o'ercharg'd cannon,
Shall I never fly in pieces? Come: to what prison?

77–78; 79–80 see Critical Notes.
78 *scourge-stick* whip for a top
91 *what a* Q1b (Q1a what).          S.D. Q1b (Q1a [omits])
94 *move* Q1b (Q1a more)          95 *adventure* quarry (Lucas)
97 see Critical Notes on III,v, 79–80.
98 speech-prefix: Q1b *Bos.* (Q1a [omits])
102 speech-prefix: Q1b *Duch.* (Q1a *Ant.*); *o'ercharg'd* ed. (Q1
    orechar'd; Q2, Q3 ore-charg'd; Q4 [omits])

*Bosola.* To none.
*Duchess.*                    Whither then?
*Bosola.*                                To your palace.
105   *Duchess.* I have heard that Charon's boat serves to convey
All o'er the dismal lake, but brings none back again.
*Bosola.* Your brothers mean you safety and pity.
*Duchess.* Pity!
With such a pity men preserve alive
110   Pheasants and quails, when they are not fat enough
To be eaten.
*Bosola.* These are your children?
*Duchess.*                              Yes.
*Bosola.*                                      Can they prattle?
*Duchess.* No:
But I intend, since they were born accurs'd;
Curses shall be their first language.
115   *Bosola.*                            Fie, Madam!
Forget this base, low fellow.
*Duchess.*                        Were I a man,
I'll'd beat that counterfeit face into thy other—
*Bosola.* One of no birth.
*Duchess.*                        Say that he was born mean,
Man is most happy, when's own actions
120   Be arguments and examples of his virtue.
*Bosola.* A barren, beggarly virtue.
*Duchess.* I prithee, who is greatest, can you tell?
Sad tales befit my woe: I'll tell you one.
A Salmon, as she swam unto the sea,
125   Met with a Dog-fish; who encounters her
With this rough language: 'Why art thou so bold
To mix thyself with our our high state of floods
Being no eminent courtier, but one
That for the calmest and fresh time o'th' year
130   Dost live in shallow rivers, rank'st thyself
With silly Smelts and Shrimps? And darest thou
Pass by our Dog-ship without reverence?'
'O', quoth the Salmon, 'sister, be at peace:
Thank Jupiter, we both have pass'd the Net,
135   Our value never can be truly known,

109 *such a* Q1b (Q1a such)
117 *counterfeit face* i.e. the vizard
122–138 Although both compositors make frequent use of them,
    in this speech the capitals serve to stress the meaning of
    the parable. They have, therefore, been preserved except
    in Sea, Courtier and Rivers. See Critical Introduction, p. xxi.

Till in the Fisher's basket we be shown;
I'th' Market then my price may be the higher,
Even when I am nearest to the Cook, and fire.
So, to great men, the moral may be stretched.
*Men oft are valued high, when th'are most wretch'd.*                    140
But come: whither you please. I am arm'd 'gainst misery:
Bent to all sways of the oppressor's will.
*There's no deep valley, but near some great hill.*    *Ex[eunt.]*

## Act IV, Scene i

[*Enter* FERDINAND *and* BOSOLA.]

*Ferdinand.* How doth our sister Duchess bear herself
In her imprisonment?
*Bosola.*            Nobly: I'll describe her:
She's sad, as one long us'd to't: and she seems
Rather to welcome the end of misery
Than shun it: a behaviour so noble,                                     5
As gives a majesty to adversity:
You may discern the shape of loveliness
More perfect in her tears, than in her smiles;
She will muse four hours together: and her silence,
Methinks, expresseth more than if she spake.                           10
*Ferdinand.* Her melancholy seems to be fortifi'd
With a strange disdain.
*Bosola.*              'Tis so: and this restraint
(Like English mastives, that grow fierce with tying)
Makes her too passionately apprehend
Those pleasures she's kept from.
*Ferdinand.*                    Curse upon her!                         15
I will no longer study in the book
Of another's heart: inform her what I told you.    *Exit.*
[BOSOLA *draws the traverse to reveal the* DUCHESS, CARIOLA *and*
SERVANTS.]
*Bosola.* All comfort to your Grace;—
*Duchess.*                    I will have none.
'Pray-thee, why dost thou wrap thy poison'd pills
In gold and sugar?                                                     20
*Bosola.* Your elder brother the Lord Ferdinand
Is come to visit you: and sends you word

143 i.e. in depression one finds a source of strength nearby: *cf.*
    Psalm cxxi.
3  *long us'd* Q1 (Q2, Q3, Q4 us'd)
21 *elder brother:* historically accurate; but in the play this is only
    Bosola's impression *cf.* IV,ii, 261–3.

'Cause once he rashly made a solemn vow
Never to see you more; he comes i'th' night;
25    And prays you, gently, neither torch nor taper
Shine in your chamber: he will kiss your hand;
And reconcile himself: but, for his vow,
He dares not see you.
    *Duchess.*          At his pleasure.
Take hence the lights: he's come.
    [*Exeunt* SERVANTS *with lights*; *enter* FERDINAND.]
    *Ferdinand.*           Where are you?
    *Duchess.*                    Here sir.
    *Ferdinand.* This darkness suits you well.
30        *Duchess.*           I would ask your pardon.
    *Ferdinand.* You have it;
For I account it the honorabl'st revenge
Where I may kill, to pardon: where are your cubs?
    *Duchess.* Whom?
35        *Ferdinand.* Call them your children;
For though our national law distinguish bastards
From true legitimate issue, compassionate nature
Makes them all equal.
    *Duchess.*          Do you visit me for this?
You violate a sacrament o'th' Church
Shall make you howl in hell for't.
40        *Ferdinand.*          It had been well,
Could you have liv'd thus always: for indeed
You were too much i'th' light. But no more;
I come to seal my peace with you: here's a hand,
                 (*gives her a dead man's hand.*)
To which you have vow'd much love: the ring upon't
You gave.
45        *Duchess.* I affectionately kiss it.
    *Ferdinand.* Pray do: and bury the print of it in your
                          heart.
I will leave this ring with you, for a love-token:
And the hand, as sure as the ring: and do not doubt
But you shall have the heart too. When you need a friend
50    Send it to him that ow'd it: you shall see
Whether he can aid you.
    *Duchess.*          You are very cold.

39 *a sacrament o'th' Church* see Critical Notes.
42 *i'th' light* in the public gaze      43 S.D. see Critical Notes.
44–5 *the ring upon't You gave* i.e. her wedding ring, torn off by the
      Cardinal
50 *ow'd* owned.

I fear you are not well after your travel:
Ha! Lights: Oh horrible!
   *Ferdinand.*            Let her have lights enough. [*Exit.*
[*Enter* SERVANTS *with lights.*]
   *Duchess.* What witchcraft doth he practise, that he hath
                                     left
A dead man's hand here?—                                                    55

*Here is discover'd, behind a traverse, the artificial figures of*
ANTONIO *and his children; appearing as if they were dead.*

   *Bosola.* Look you: here's the piece from which 'twas tane;
He doth present you this sad spectacle,
That now you know directly they are dead,
Hereafter you may, wisely, cease to grieve
For that which cannot be recovered.                                         60
   *Duchess.* There is not between heaven and earth one wish
I stay for after this: it wastes me more,
Than were't my picture, fashion'd out of wax,
Stuck with a magical needle, and then buried
In some foul dunghill: and yond's an excellent property    65
For a tyrant, which I would account mercy,—
   *Bosola.* What's that?
   *Duchess.* If they would bind me to that lifeless trunk,
And let me freeze to death.
   *Bosola.*            Come, you must live.
   *Duchess.* That's the greatest torture souls feel in hell,   70
In hell: that they must live, and cannot die.
Portia, I'll new kindle thy coals again,
And revive the rare and almost dead example
Of a loving wife.
   *Bosola.*        O fie! despair? remember
You are a Christian.
   *Duchess.*        The Church enjoins fasting:            75
I'll starve myself to death.
   *Bosola.*           Leave this vain sorrow;
Things being at the worst, begin to mend:
The bee when he hath shot his sting into your hand
May then play with your eyelid.

---

S.D. *behind* Q1 (Q2, Q3 *being*; Q4 [omits]); *children* see
     Critical Notes.
58 *directly* straightforwardly
61 *earth* Q1, Q4 (Q2, Q3 the earth)
72 *Portia,* wife of Brutus, choked by keeping hot coals in her
     mouth after hearing of her husband's defeat and suicide
     at Philippi.

*Duchess.*            Good comfortable fellow
80 Persuade a wretch that's broke upon the wheel
To have all his bones new set: entreat him live,
To be executed again. Who must dispatch me?
I account this world a tedious theatre,
For I do play a part in't 'gainst my will.
85    *Bosola.* Come, be of comfort, I will save your life.
*Duchess.* Indeed I have not leisure to tend so small a
                              business.

*Bosola.* Now, by my life, I pity you.
*Duchess.*             Thou art a fool then,
To waste thy pity on a thing so wretch'd
As cannot pity itself. I am full of daggers.
90 Puff! let me blow these vipers from me.  [*Enter* SERVANT.]
What are you?
*Servant.*    One that wishes you long life.
*Duchess.* I would thou wert hang'd for the horrible curse
Thou hast given me: I shall shortly grow one
Of the miracles of pity. I'll go pray. No,
I'll go curse.
   *Bosola.*    Oh fie!
95    *Duchess.*         I could curse the stars.
*Bosola.* Oh fearful!
*Duchess.* And those three smiling seasons of the year
Into a Russian winter: nay the world
To its first chaos.
   *Bosola.* Look you, the stars shine still.
*Duchess.*             Oh, but you must
100 Remember, my curse hath a great way to go:
Plagues, that make lanes through largest families,
Consume them.
   *Bosola.*      Fie lady!
   *Duchess.*      Let them like tyrants
Never be rememb'red, but for the ill they have done:
Let all the zealous prayers of mortified
Churchmen forget them,—
105    *Bosola.*           O uncharitable!
*Duchess.* Let Heaven, a little while, cease crowning
                               martyrs
To punish them.
Go, howl them this: and say I long to bleed.
*It is some mercy when men kill with speed.*
                         *Exit* [*with* SERVANTS.]

[*Enter* FERDINAND.]

89 *itself* Q4 (Q1, Q2, Q3 it)

*Ferdinand.* Excellent; as I would wish: she plagu'd in
art.  110
These presentations are but fram'd in wax
By the curious master in that quality,
Vincentio Lauriola, and she takes them
For true substantial bodies.
    *Bosola.*               Why do you do this?
    *Ferdinand.* To bring her to despair.
    *Bosola.*                  'Faith, end here;  115
And go no farther in your cruelty,
Send her a penitential garment, to put on
Next to her delicate skin, and furnish her
With beads and prayerbooks.
    *Ferdinand.*        Damn her! that body of hers,
While that my blood ran pure in't, was more worth  120
Than that which thou wouldst comfort, call'd a soul.
I will send her masques of common courtesans,
Have her meat serv'd up by bawds and ruffians,
And, 'cause she'll needs be mad, I am resolv'd
To remove forth the common hospital  125
All the mad folk, and place them near her lodging:
There let them practise together, sing, and dance,
And act their gambols to the full o'th' moon:
If she can sleep the better for it, let her.
Your work is almost ended.
    *Bosola.*          Must I see her again?  130
    *Ferdinand.* Yes.
    *Bosola.*        Never.
    *Ferdinand.*       You must.
    *Bosola.*             Never in mine own shape;
That's forfeited by my intelligence,
And this last cruel lie: when you send me next,
The business shall be comfort.
    *Ferdinand.*       Very likely:
Thy pity is nothing of kin to thee. Antonio  135
Lurks about Milan; thou shalt shortly thither,
To feed a fire as great as my revenge,
Which nev'r will slack, till it have spent his fuel;
*Intemperate agues make physicians cruel.*

                             *Exeunt.*

115 '*Faith* i'faith, a common interjection of 16th–17th centuries
117 *penitential garment* see Critical Notes.
125 *remove forth* remove forth from
132 *by my intelligence* by my acting as intelligencer
133 *cruel lie* Q1, Q2 (Q3, Q4 cruelty)

## Scene ii

[*Enter* DUCHESS *and* CARIOLA.]

*Duchess.* What hideous noise was that?
*Cariola.*                           'Tis the wild consort
Of madmen, lady, which your tyrant brother
Hath plac'd about your lodging. This tyranny,
I think, was never practis'd till this hour.
5      *Duchess.* Indeed I thank him: nothing but noise, and folly
Can keep me in my right wits, whereas reason
And silence make me stark mad. Sit down,
Discourse to me some dismal tragedy.
*Cariola.* O 'twill increase your melancholy.
*Duchess.*                           Thou art deceiv'd;
10   To hear of greater grief would lessen mine.
This is a prison?
*Cariola.*          Yes, but you shall live
To shake this durance off.
*Duchess.*                 Thou art a fool:
The robin red-breast and the nightingale
Never live long in cages.
*Cariola.*               Pray dry your eyes.
15   What think you of Madam?
*Duchess.* Of nothing:
When I muse thus, I sleep.
*Cariola.* Like a madman, with your eyes open?
*Duchess.* Dost thou think we shall know one another
In th'other world?
20     *Cariola.*          Yes, out of question.
*Duchess.* O that it were possible we might
But hold some two days' conference with the dead,
From them I should learn somewhat, I am sure
I never shall know here. I'll tell thee a miracle,
25   I am not mad yet, to my cause of sorrow.
Th'heaven o'er my head seems made of molten brass,
The earth of flaming sulphur, yet I am not mad.
I am acquainted with sad misery,
As the tann'd galley-slave is with his oar.
30   Necessity makes me suffer constantly.
And custom makes it easy. Who do I look like now?

1 *consort* collection of musicians who sing and play together

*Cariola.* Like to your picture in the gallery,
A deal of life in show, but none in practice:
Or rather like some reverend monument
Whose ruins are even pitied.
*Duchess.*                    Very proper:          35
And Fortune seems only to have her eyesight,
To behold my tragedy.
How now! what noise is that?        [*Enter* SERVANT.]
*Servant.*                 I am come to tell you,
Your brother hath intended you some sport.
A great physician when the Pope was sick          40
Of a deep melancholy, presented him
With several sorts of madmen, which wild object,
Being full of change and sport, forc'd him to laugh,
And so th'imposthume broke: the selfsame cure
The Duke intends on you.
*Duchess.*               Let them come in.          45
*Servant.* There's a mad lawyer, and a secular priest,
A doctor that hath forfeited his wits
By jealousy; an astrologian,
That in his works said such a day o'th' month
Should be the day of doom; and, failing of't,          50
Ran mad; an English tailor, craz'd i'th' brain
With the study of new fashion; a gentleman usher
Quite beside himself with care to keep in mind
The number of his lady's salutations,
Or 'How do you?' she employ'd him in each morning:          55
A farmer too, an excellent knave in grain,
Mad, 'cause he was hind'red transportation;
And let one broker, that's mad, loose to these,
You'ld think the devil were among them.
*Duchess.* Sit Cariola: let them loose when you please,          60
For I am chain'd to endure all your tyranny.

[*Enter* MADMEN.]

*Here, by a madman, this song is sung to a dismal kind of music.*

    *O let us howl, some heavy note,*
        *some deadly-dogged howl,*

44 *imposthume* abscess        45 *them* Q1 (Q4 'em; Q2, Q3 me)
46 *secular priest* one not belonging to a monastic order
52 *fashion* Q1 (Q2, Q3, Q4 fashions)
56 *knave in grain* a knave in the grain trade; an ingrained knave
57 *transportation* export        58 *broker* pawnbroker
60–61 A reference to the chaining up of mad people *cf.* I,ii, 337–8.

*Sounding, as from the threat'ning throat,*
65     *of beasts, and fatal fowl.*
*As ravens, screech-owls, bulls, and bears,*
*We'll bell, and bawl our parts,*
*Till yerksome noise, have cloy'd your ears,*
*and corrosiv'd your hearts.*
70     *At last when as our quire wants breath,*
*our bodies being blest,*
*We'll sing like swans, to welcome death,*
*and die in love and rest.*

*Mad Astrologer.* Doomsday not come yet? I'll draw it
75     nearer by a perspective, or make a glass, that shall set all the
world on fire upon an instant. I cannot sleep, my pillow is
stufft with a litter of porcupines.

*Mad Lawyer.* Hell is a mere glass-house, where the devils
are continually blowing up women's souls on hollow irons,
80     and the fire never goes out.

*Mad Priest.* I will lie with every woman in my parish
the tenth night: I will tithe them over like haycocks.

*Mad Doctor.* Shall my pothecary outgo me, because I am
a cuckold? I have found out his roguery: he makes allum of
85     his wife's urine, and sells it to Puritans, that have sore
throats with over-straining.

*Mad Astrologer.* I have skill in heraldry.

*Mad Lawyer.* Hast?

*Mad Astrologer.* You do give for your crest a woodcock's
90     head, with the brains pick'd out on't. You are a very ancient
gentleman.

*Mad Priest.* Greek is turn'd Turk; we are only to be sav'd
by the Helvetian translation.

*Mad Astrologer [to* LAWYER]. Come on sir, I will lay the
95     law to you.

*Mad Lawyer.* Oh, rather lay a corrosive, the law will eat
to the bone.

*Mad Priest.* He that drinks but to satisfy nature is damn'd.

62–73 The punctuation suggests pauses in the music, and, there-
    fore the style of singing.
66 *bears* ed. (Q1, Q2 Beares; Q3, Q4 Bares)
67 *bell* Q2, Q3, Q4 bellow (Q1 bill)
68 *yerksome* Q1, Q2, Q3 (Q4 irksome)
69 *corrosiv'd* Q4 corroded (Q1, Q2, Q3 corasiv'd)
75 *perspective* telescope          78 *glass-house* glass factory
79 *women's* Q1 (Q2, Q3, Q4 men's)
89 the woodcock was considered to be brainless
92–3 see Critical Notes.          94–5 *lay the law* expound the law
96 *lay a corrosive* apply a corrosive

*Mad Doctor.* If I had my glass here, I would show a sight
should make all the women here call me mad doctor.                    100

*Mad Astrologer* [*pointing to* PRIEST]. What's he, a ropemaker?

*Mad Lawyer.* No, no, no, a snuffling knave, that while he
shows the tombs, will have his hand in a wench's placket.

*Mad Priest.* Woe to the caroche that brought home my      105
wife from the masque, at three o'clock in the morning; it
had a large feather bed in it.

*Mad Doctor.* I have pared the devil's nails forty times,
roasted them in raven's eggs, and cur'd agues with them.

*Mad Priest.* Get me three hundred milch bats, to make      110
possets to procure sleep.

*Mad Doctor.* All the college may throw their caps at me, I
have made a soap-boiler costive: it was my masterpiece:—

*Here the dance consisting of 8. madmen, with music answerable
thereunto, after which* BOSOLA, *like an old man, enters.*

*Duchess.* Is he mad too?
*Servant.*                          Pray question him; I'll leave you.
                    [*Exeunt* SERVANT *and* MADMEN.]
*Bosola.* I am come to make thy tomb.
*Duchess.*                          Ha! my tomb?                    115
Thou speak'st as if I lay upon my death-bed,
Gasping for breath: dost thou perceive me sick?
*Bosola.* Yes, and the more dangerously, since thy sickness
is insensible.
*Duchess.* Thou art not mad, sure; dost know me?          120
*Bosola.* Yes.
*Duchess.* Who am I?
*Bosola.* Thou art a box of worm seed, at best, but a sal-
vatory of green mummy: what's this flesh? a little cruded
milk, fantastical puff-paste: our bodies are weaker than those   125
paper prisons boys use to keep flies in: more contemptible;

101–2 *ropemaker* i.e. in league with the hangman
111 *possets*, made with hot milk curdled with ale or wine and with
        spices added
112 *throw their caps at* they may do their utmost against me but it
        will be in vain (Lucas)
113 *costive* constipated
S.D. *like an old man* Q1, Q2, Q3, (Q4 *like an Old Bell-Man*)
119 *insensible* imperceptible
123–4 *salvatory* ointment box
124 *mummy* mummia, a medicinal preparation made from Egyp-
        tian mummies; *cruded* curdled
125 *puff-paste* one of the lightest types of pastry, containing a lot
        of air

since ours is to preserve earth-worms: didst thou ever see
a lark in a cage? such is the soul in the body: this world
is like her little turf of grass, and the heaven o'er our heads,
130  like her looking-glass, only gives us a miserable knowledge
of the small compass of our prison.
　　　*Duchess.* Am not I thy Duchess?
　　　*Bosola.* Thou art some great woman, sure; for riot begins
to sit on thy forehead (clad in grey hairs) twenty years sooner
135  than on a merry milkmaid's. Thou sleep'st worse, than if a
mouse should be forc'd to take up her lodging in a cat's ear:
a little infant, that breeds its teeth, should it lie with thee,
would cry out, as if thou wert the more unquiet bedfellow.
　　　*Duchess.* I am Duchess of Malfi still.
140  　　*Bosola.* That makes thy sleeps so broken:
*Glories, like glow-worms, afar off shine bright,*
*But look'd to near, have neither heat nor light.*
　　　*Duchess.* Thou art very plain.
　　　*Bosola.* My trade is to flatter the dead, not the living;
145  I am a tomb-maker.
　　　*Duchess.* And thou com'st to make my tomb?
　　　*Bosola.* Yes.
　　　*Duchess.* Let me be a little merry;
Of what stuff wilt thou make it?
150  　　*Bosola.* Nay, resolve me first, of what fashion?
　　　*Duchess.* Why, do we grow fantastical in our death-bed?
Do we affect fashion in the grave?
　　　*Bosola.* Most ambitiously. Princes' images on their tombs
Do not lie as they were wont, seeming to pray
155  Up to Heaven: but with their hands under their cheeks,
As if they died of the tooth-ache; they are not carved
With their eyes fix'd upon the stars; but as
Their minds were wholly bent upon the world,
The self-same way they seem to turn their faces.
160  　　*Duchess.* Let me know fully therefore the effect
Of this thy dismal preparation,
This talk, fit for a charnel.
　　　*Bosola.*　　　　　　　Now I shall;

[*Enter* EXECUTIONERS *with*] *a coffin, cords, and a bell.*

Here is a present from your princely brothers,

---

126 *ever* Q1 (Q2, Q3, Q4 never)
136 *her* Q1 (Q2, Q3, Q4 his)
140 *sleeps* Q1, Q2 (Q3, Q4 sleep)
142 *to* Q1, Q3 (Q2 too; Q4 on)　　　　　　　150 *resolve* explain
162 *charnel* Q1, Q4 (Q2 chamell; Q3 chamel)

And may it arrive welcome, for it brings
Last benefit, last sorrow.
*Duchess.*                    Let me see it.                    165
I have so much obedience, in my blood,
I wish it in their veins, to do them good.
*Bosola.* This is your last presence chamber.
*Cariola.* O my sweet lady!
*Duchess.*                    Peace; it affrights not me.
*Bosola.* I am the common bellman,                            170
That usually is sent to condemn'd persons,
The night before they suffer.
*Duchess.*                    Even now thou said'st
Thou wast a tomb-maker?
*Bosola.*                    'Twas to bring you
By degrees to mortification. Listen:          [*rings the bell*]
 *Hark, now every thing is still,*                        175
 *The screech-owl and the whistler shrill*
 *Call upon our Dame, aloud,*
 *And bid her quickly don her shroud.*
 *Much you had of land and rent,*
 *Your length in clay's now competent.*                    180
 *A long war disturb'd your mind,*
 *Here your perfect peace is sign'd.*
 *Of what is't fools make such vain keeping?*
 *Sin their conception, their birth, weeping:*
 *Their life, a general mist of error,*                    185
 *Their death, a hideous storm of terror.*
 *Strew your hair with powders sweet:*
 *Don clean linen, bath your feet,*
 *And, the foul fiend more to check,*
 *A crucifix let bless your neck.*                         190
 *'Tis now full tide 'tween night and day,*
 *End your groan, and come away.*

[EXECUTIONERS *approach.*]

*Cariola.* Hence villains, tyrants, murderers. Alas!
What will you do with my lady? Call for help.

176 *whistler* a bird with a whistling cry, the hearing of which is
   considered an ill omen
179 *rent* revenue, income
180 *competent* sufficient in means for comfortable living
182 *peace* treaty; *quietus cf.* I,ii, 380.
183 *keeping* taking care of; defending; retaining
186 *terror* Q1, Q4 (Q2, Q3 error)
188 *bath* Q1, Q4 (Q2, Q3 bathe)
190 *A crucifix let bless* 'Let a crucifix make the sign of the cross on'.

*Duchess.* To whom, to our next neighbours? They are
195                                                   mad-folks.
*Bosola.* Remove that noise.
              [EXECUTIONERS *seize* CARIOLA, *who struggles.*]
*Duchess.*                            Farewell Cariola,
In my last will I have not much to give;
A many hungry guests have fed upon me,
Thine will be a poor reversion.
      *Cariola.*                    I will die with her.
200   *Duchess.* I pray thee look thou giv'st my little boy
Some syrup for his cold, and let the girl
Say her prayers, ere she sleep.       [CARIOLA *is forced off.*]
                              Now what you please,
What death?
      *Bosola.* Strangling: here are your executioners.
      *Duchess.* I forgive them:
205   The apoplexy, catarrh, or cough o'th' lungs
Would do as much as they do.
      *Bosola.* Doth not death fright you?
      *Duchess.*                    Who would be afraid on't?
Knowing to meet such excellent company
In th'other world.
      *Bosola.*            Yet, methinks,
210   The manner of your death should much afflict you,
This cord should terrify you?
      *Duchess.*                    Not a whit:
What would it pleasure me, to have my throat cut
With diamonds? or to be smothered
With cassia? or to be shot to death, with pearls?
215   I know death hath ten thousand several doors
For men to take their *Exits*: and 'tis found
They go on such strange geometrical hinges,
You may open them both ways: any way, for Heaven sake,
So I were out of your whispering. Tell my brothers
220   That I perceive death, now I am well awake,
Best gift is, they can give, or I can take.
I would fain put off my last woman's fault,
I'll'd not be tedious to you.
      *Executioners.*             We are ready.
      *Duchess.* Dispose my breath how please you, but my body
Bestow upon my women, will you?
225   *Executioners.*                    Yes.

199 *reversion* something succeeded to upon the death of the holder
205 *catarrh* cerebral effusion or haemorrhage
217–8 see Critical Notes on III,v, 79–80.

*Duchess.* Pull, and pull strongly, for your able strength
Must pull down heaven upon me:
Yet stay, heaven gates are not so highly arch'd
As princes' palaces: they that enter there
Must go upon their knees. Come violent death,                    230
Serve for mandragora to make me sleep;
Go tell my brothers, when I am laid out,
They then may feed in quiet.            *They strangle her.*
   *Bosola.*                        Where's the waiting woman?
Fetch her. Some other strangle the children.
         [*Exeunt* EXECUTIONERS. *Enter one with* CARIOLA.]
Look you, there sleeps your mistress.                            235
   *Cariola.*                       O you are damn'd
Perpetually for this. My turn is next,
Is't not so ordered?
   *Bosola.*            Yes, and I am glad
You are so well prepar'd for't.
   *Cariola.*                     You are deceiv'd sir,
I am not prepar'd for't. I will not die,
I will first come to my answer; and know                         240
How I have offended.
   *Bosola.*            Come, dispatch her.
You kept her counsel, now you shall keep ours.
   *Cariola.* I will not die, I must not, I am contracted
To a young gentleman.
   *Executioner* [*showing the noose*]. Here's your wedding-ring.
   *Cariola.* Let me but speak with the Duke. I'll discover       245
Treason to his person.
   *Bosola.*            Delays: throttle her.
   *Executioner.* She bites: and scratches.
   *Cariola.*                    If you kill me now
I am damn'd. I have not been at confession
This two years.
   *Bosola.*     When!
   *Cariola.*         I am quick with child.
   *Bosola.*                             Why then,
Your credit's sav'd: bear her into th' next room.                250

229 *princes' palaces* Q1 (Q2, Q3, Q4 princely palaces)
231 *mandragora* the mandrake plant, taken by the Elizabethans to
       be a type of narcotic
235 *you are* Q1 (Q2, Q3, Q4 thou art)
237 *and I am glad* Q1 (Q2, Q3, Q4 I am glad)
240 *I will first come . . .* Q1 (Q2, Q3 I will come . . .; Q4 I will
       come to my Tryal)
249 *When!* see II,i, 117 note.
250 *th' next* Q1, Q2 (Q3, Q4 the next)

Let this lie still.
[EXECUTIONERS *strangle* CARIOLA *and exeunt with her body.*
*Enter* FERDINAND.]

    *Ferdinand.*   Is she dead?
    *Bosola.*             She is what
You'll'd have her. But here begin your pity,
[BOSOLA *draws the traverse and*] *Shows the children strangled.*
Alas, how have these offended?
    *Ferdinand.*           The death
Of young wolves is never to be pitied.
    *Bosola.* Fix your eye here.
    *Ferdinand.*          Constantly.
255    *Bosola.*                Do you not weep?
Other sins only speak; murther shrieks out:
The element of water moistens the earth,
But blood flies upwards, and bedews the heavens.
    *Ferdinand.* Cover her face. Mine eyes dazzle: she di'd
                               young.
260    *Bosola.* I think not so: her infelicity
Seem'd to have years too many.
    *Ferdinand.*         She and I were twins:
And should I die this instant, I had liv'd
Her time to a minute.
    *Bosola.*        It seems she was born first:
You have bloodily approv'd the ancient truth,
265   That kindred commonly do worse agree
Than remote strangers.
    *Ferdinand.*      Let me see her face again;
Why didst not thou pity her? What an excellent
Honest man might'st thou have been
If thou hadst borne her to some sanctuary!
270   Or, bold in a good cause, oppos'd thyself
With thy advanced sword above thy head,
Between her innocence and my revenge!
I bad thee, when I was distracted of my wits,
Go kill my dearest friend, and thou hast done't.
275   For let me but examine well the cause;
What was the meanness of her match to me?
Only I must confess, I had a hope,
Had she continu'd widow, to have gain'd

259 *di'd* Q1, Q2, Q3 (Q4 died)
264 *approv'd* confirmed, demonstrated
272 *innocence* Q1, Q4 (Q2, Q3 innocency)
274 *done't* ed. (Qq. don't)

An infinite mass of treasure by her death:
And that was the main cause; her marriage,                    280
That drew a stream of gall quite through my heart;
For thee, (as we observe in tragedies
That a good actor many times is curs'd
For playing a villain's part) I hate thee for't:
And, for my sake, say thou hast done much ill, well.          285
    *Bosola.* Let me quicken your memory: for I perceive
You are falling into ingratitude. I challenge
The reward due to my service.
    *Ferdinand.*               I'll tell thee,
What I'll give thee—
    *Bosola.*        Do.
    *Ferdinand.*           I'll give thee a pardon
For this murther.
    *Bosola.*     Ha?
    *Ferdinand.*       Yes: and 'tis                        290
The largest bounty I can study to do thee.
By what authority didst thou execute
This bloody sentence?
    *Bosola.*        By yours.
    *Ferdinand.*             Mine? Was I her judge?
Did any ceremonial form of law
Doom her to not-being? did a complete jury                    295
Deliver her conviction up i'th' court?
Where shalt thou find this judgment register'd
Unless in hell? See: like a bloody fool
Th'hast forfeited thy life, and thou shalt die for't.
    *Bosola.* The office of justice is perverted quite              300
When one thief hangs another: who shall dare
To reveal this?
    *Ferdinand.*  Oh, I'll tell thee:
The wolf shall find her grave, and scrape it up;
Not to devour the corpse, but to discover
The horrid murther.
    *Bosola.*        You; not I shall quake for't.              305
    *Ferdinand.* Leave me.
    *Bosola.*          I will first receive my pension.
    *Ferdinand.* You are a villain.
    *Bosola.*           When your ingratitude
Is judge, I am so—
    *Ferdinand.*    O horror!

280 *And that was the main cause;* Q1 (Q2 And what was the main
        cause; Q3, Q4 And what was the main cause )
293 *sentence* Q1 (Q2, Q3, Q4 service)

That not the fear of him which binds the devils
310    Can prescribe man obedience.
Never look upon me more.
    *Bosola.*              Why fare thee well:
Your brother and yourself are worthy men;
You have a pair of hearts are hollow graves,
Rotten, and rotting others: and your vengeance,
315    Like two chain'd bullets, still goes arm in arm;
You may be brothers: for treason, like the plague,
Doth take much in a blood. I stand like one
That long hath tane a sweet and golden dream.
I am angry with myself, now that I wake.
320        *Ferdinand.* Get thee into some unknown part o'th' world
That I may never see thee.
    *Bosola.*          Let me know
Wherefore I should be thus neglected? Sir,
I served your tyranny: and rather strove
To satisfy yourself, than all the world;
325    And though I loath'd the evil, yet I lov'd
You that did counsel it: and rather sought
To appear a true servant than an honest man.
    *Ferdinand.* I'll go hunt the badger by owl-light:
'Tis a deed of darkness.                  *Exit.*
330        *Bosola.* He's much distracted. Off my painted honour!
While with vain hopes our faculties we tire,
We seem to sweat in ice and freeze in fire;
What would I do, were this to do again?
I would not change my peace of conscience
335    For all the wealth of Europe. She stirs; here's life.
Return, fair soul, from darkness, and lead mine
Out of this sensible hell. She's warm, she breathes:
Upon thy pale lips I will melt my heart
To store them with fresh colour. Who's there?
340    Some cordial drink! Alas! I dare not call:
So pity would destroy pity: her eye opes,
And heaven in it seems to ope, that late was shut,
To take me up to mercy.
    *Duchess.*          Antonio!
    *Bosola.* Yes, Madam, he is living,

317 *take much in a blood* take much effect by families
330 *painted honour* see Critical Notes.
337 *sensible* perceptible, palpable
340 *cordial* heart-strengthening
341 *opes* Q1, Q2 (Q3, Q4 opens)
342 *ope* Q1, Q2 (Q3, Q4 open)
343 *mercy* Q2, Q3, Q4 (Q1 merry)

The dead bodies you saw were but feign'd statues;            345
He's reconcil'd to your brothers: the Pope hath wrought
The atonement.
    *Duchess.*    Mercy.                *she dies.*
    *Bosola.* Oh, she's gone again: there the cords of life
                                broke.
Oh sacred innocence, that sweetly sleeps
On turtles' feathers: whilst a guilty conscience            350
Is a black register, wherein is writ
All our good deeds and bad; a perspective
That shows us hell; that we cannot be suffer'd
To do good when we have a mind to it!
This is manly sorrow:                                        355
These tears, I am very certain, never grew
In my mother's milk. My estate is sunk
Below the degree of fear: where were
These penitent fountains while she was living?
Oh, they were frozen up: here is a sight                     360
As direful to my soul as is the sword
Unto a wretch hath slain his father. Come,
I'll bear thee hence,
And execute thy last will; that's deliver
Thy body to the reverend dispose                            365
Of some good women: that the cruel tyrant
Shall not deny me. Then I'll post to Milan,
Where somewhat I will speedily enact
Worth my dejection.        *Exit [carrying the body.]*


### Act V, Scene i

*[Enter* ANTONIO *and* DELIO.]

    *Antonio.* What think you of my hope of reconcilement
To the Aragonian brethren?
    *Delio.*               I misdoubt it
For though they have sent their letters of safe conduct
For your repair to Milan, they appear
But nets to entrap you. The Marquis of Pescara,             5
Under whom you hold certain land in cheat,

---

347 *atonement* reconciliation
364 *thy last will* Q1 (Q2, Q3, Q4 thy will)
6 *in cheat* ed. (Q1, Q2, Q3 in Cheit; Q4 in Escheat): land thus held
    could revert to the lord from whom it was held upon the
    tenant's committing treason or other felony.

Much 'gainst his noble nature, hath been mov'd
To seize those lands, and some of his dependants
Are at this instant making it their suit
10    To be invested in your revenues.
I cannot think they mean well to your life,
That do deprive you of your means of life,
Your living.
  *Antonio.* You are still an heretic.
To any safety I can shape myself.
15      *Delio.* Here comes the Marquis. I will make myself
Petitioner for some part of your land,
To know whither it is flying.
  *Antonio.*     I pray do. [*Enter* PESCARA.]
  *Delio.* Sir, I have a suit to you.
  *Pescara.*     To me?
  *Delio.*       An easy one:
There is the citadel of St. Bennet,
20    With some demenses, of late in the possession
Of Antonio Bologna; please you bestow them on me?
  *Pescara.* You are my friend. But this is such a suit
Nor fit for me to give, nor you to take.
  *Delio.* No sir?
  *Pescara.*  I will give you ample reason for't
25    Soon, in private. Here's the Cardinal's mistress.
[*Enter* JULIA.]
  *Julia.* My lord, I am grown your poor petitioner, ·
And should be an ill beggar, had I not
A great man's letter here, the Cardinal's
To court you in my favour.
       [*She gives him a letter which he reads.*]
  *Pescara.*     He entreats for you
30    The citadel of Saint Bennet, that belong'd
To the banish'd Bologna.
  *Julia.*    Yes.
  *Pescara.* I could not have thought of a friend I could
Rather pleasure with it: 'tis yours.
  *Julia.*     Sir, I thank you:
And he shall know how doubly I am engag'd
35    Both in your gift, and speediness of giving,
Which makes your grant the greater.    *Exit.*

13 *heretic.* Q1, Q2, Q3 (Q4, Dyce, Hazlitt, Vaughan, Sampson,
  Lucas, McIlwraith: heretic)
19 *St. Bennet* St. Benedict
25 *Here's* Q1, Q4 (Q2, Q3 Her's)

*Antonio* [*aside*].               How they fortify
Themselves with my ruin!
    *Delio*.           Sir, I am
Little bound to you.
    *Pescara*.     Why?
    *Delio*. Because you deni'd this suit to me, and gave't
To such a creature.
    *Pescara*.        Do you know what it was?       40
It was Antonio's land: not forfeited
By course of law; but ravish'd from his throat
By the Cardinal's entreaty: it were not fit
I should bestow so main a piece of wrong
Upon my friend: 'tis a gratification             45
Only due to a strumpet; for it is injustice.
Shall I sprinkle the pure blood of innocents
To make those followers I call my friends
Look ruddier upon me? I am glad
This land, tane from the owner by such wrong,     50
Returns again unto so foul an use,
As salary for his lust. Learn, good Delio,
To ask noble things of me, and you shall find
I'll be a noble giver.
    *Delio*.          You instruct me well.
    *Antonio* [*aside*]. Why, here's a man, now, would fright
                               impudence    55
From sauciest beggars.
    *Pescara*.           Prince Ferdinand's come to Milan
Sick, as thy give out, of an apoplexy:
But some say 'tis a frenzy; I am going
To visit him.                           *Exit*.
    *Antonio*. 'Tis a noble old fellow:
    *Delio*. What course do you mean to take, Antonio?    60
    *Antonio*. This night I mean to venture all my fortune,
Which is no more than a poor ling'ring life,
To the Cardinal's worst of malice. I have got
Private access to his chamber: and intend
To visit him, about the mid of night,              65
As once his brother did our noble Duchess.
It may be that the sudden apprehension
Of danger (for I'll go in mine own shape)
When he shall see it fraight with love and duty,

54 *noble* Q1, Q2 (Q3, Q4 nobler)
59 In fact the Marquis of Pescara died at the age of 36.
64 *and intend* Q1, Q2 (Q3, Q4 and I intend.)
69 *fraight* fraught

70  May draw the poison out of him, and work
    A friendly reconcilement: if it fail,
    Yet it shall rid me of this infamous calling,
    For better fall once, than be ever falling.
       *Delio.* I'll second you in all danger: and, howe'er,
75  My life keeps rank with yours.
       *Antonio.* You are still my lov'd and best friend.

                                        *Exeunt.*


## Scene ii

### [*Enter* PESCARA *and* DOCTOR]

*Pescara.* Now doctor, may I visit your patient?
*Doctor.* If't please your lordship: but he's instantly
To take the air here in the gallery,
By my direction.
   *Pescara.*          Pray thee, what's his disease?
5  *Doctor.* A very pestilent disease, my lord,
They call lycanthropia.
   *Pescara.*              What's that?
I need a dictionary to't.
   *Doctor.*              I'll tell you:
In those that are possess'd with't there o'erflows
Such melancholy humour, they imagine
10  Themselves to be transformed into wolves.
Steal forth to churchyards in the dead of night,
And dig dead bodies up: as two nights since
One met the Duke, 'bout midnight in a lane
Behind St. Mark's church, with the leg of a man
15  Upon his shoulder; and he howl'd fearfully:
Said he was a wolf: only the difference
Was, a wolf's skin was hairy on the outside,
His on the inside: bad them take their swords,
Rip up his flesh, and try: straight I was sent for,
20  And having minister'd to him, found his Grace
Very well recovered.
   *Pescara.*          I am glad on't.
   *Doctor.* Yet not without some fear
Of a relapse: if he grow to his fit again
I'll go a nearer way to work with him

---

6 *lycanthropia* wolf-madness      8 *those* Q1, Q4 (Q2, Q3 these)
17 *was hairy* Q1 (Q2, Q3, Q4 is hairy)
20 *to him* Q1 (Q2, Q3, Q4 unto him) 24: Q1 (Q2, Q3, Q4 [omit])

Than ever Paracelsus dream'd of. If                                    25
They'll give me leave, I'll buffet his madness out of him.
Stand aside: he comes.

[*Enter* CARDINAL, FERDINAND, MALATESTE *and* BOSOLA, *who
remains in the background.*]

*Ferdinand.* Leave me.
*Malateste.* Why doth your lordship love this solitariness?
*Ferdinand.* Eagles commonly fly alone. They are crows,          30
daws, and starlings that flock together. Look, what's that
follows me?
*Malateste.* Nothing, my lord.
*Ferdinand.* Yes.
*Malateste.* 'Tis your shadow.                                          35
*Ferdinand.* Stay it; let it not haunt me.
*Malateste.* Impossible, if you move, and the sun shine.
*Ferdinand.* I will throttle it.
                           [*Throws himself upon his shadow.*]
*Malateste.* Oh, my lord: you are angry with nothing.
*Ferdinand.* You are a fool. How is't possible I should          40
catch my shadow unless I fall upon't? When I go to hell, I
mean to carry a bribe: for look you, good gifts evermore
make way for the worst persons.
*Pescara.* Rise, good my lord.
*Ferdinand.* I am studying the art of patience.                       45
*Pescara.* 'Tis a noble virtue;—
*Ferdinand.* To drive six snails before me, from this town
to Moscow; neither use goad nor whip to them, but let
them take their own time: (the patient'st man i'th' world
match me for an experiment!) and I'll crawl after like a         50
sheep-biter.
*Cardinal.* Force him up. [*They get* FERDINAND *to his feet.*]
*Ferdinand.* Use me well, you were best.
What I have done, I have done: I'll confess nothing.
*Doctor.* Now let me come to him. Are you mad, my lord?        55
Are you out of your princely wits?
*Ferdinand.*                       What's he?
*Pescara.*                                      Your doctor.
*Ferdinand.* Let me have his beard saw'd off, and his eye-
                                                          brows
Fil'd more civil.

25 *Paracelsus* Q3 (Q1, Q2 Paraclesus; Q4 [omits])
29 *love* Q1 (Q2, Q3, Q4 use)
51 *sheep-biter* a dog that worries or bites sheep; a sneaking thief
58 *Fil'd* ed. (Q1, Q4 fil'd; Q2, Q3, fill'd); *more civil* more polite

*Doctor.* I must do mad tricks with him,
For that's the only way on't. I have brought
60 Your Grace a salamander's skin, to keep you
From sun-burning.
*Ferdinand.* I have cruel sore eyes.
*Doctor.* The white of a cocatrice's egg is present remedy.
*Ferdinand.* Let it be a new-laid one, you were best.
Hide me from him. Physicians are like kings,
They brook no contradiction.
65 *Doctor.* Now he begins
To fear me; now let me alone with him.

[FERDINAND *tries to take off his gown;* CARDINAL *seizes him.*]

*Cardinal.* How now, put off your gown?
*Doctor.* Let me have some forty urinals filled with rose-
water: he and I'll go pelt one another with them; now he
70 begins to fear me. Can you fetch a frisk, sir? [*aside to*
CARDINAL] Let him go, let him go upon my peril. I find by
his eye, he stands in awe of me: I'll make him as tame as a
dormouse. [CARDINAL *releases* FERDINAND.]
*Ferdinand.* Can you fetch your frisks, sir! I will stamp him
75 into a cullis; flay off his skin, to cover one of the anatomies,
this rogue hath set i'th' cold yonder, in Barber-Chirur-
geons' Hall. Hence, hence! you are all of you like beasts for
sacrifice, [*throws the* DOCTOR *down and beats him*] there's
nothing left of you, but tongue and belly, flattery and
80 lechery. [*Exit.*]
*Pescara.* Doctor, he did not fear you throughly.
*Doctor.* True, I was somewhat too forward.
*Bosola* [*aside*]. Mercy upon me, what a fatal judgment
Hath fall'n upon this Ferdinand!
*Pescara.* Knows your Grace
85 What accident hath brought unto the Prince
This strange distraction?
*Cardinal* [*aside*]. I must feign somewhat. Thus they say it
grew:

62 *present* immediate    70 *fetch a frisk* cut a caper
75 *cullis* cf. II, iv, 66 n.; *anatomies* Q2, Q3, Q4 (Q1 anotomies)
    skeletons used in anatomical studies
76-77 *Barber–Chirurgeons' Hall* contained an anatomical museum.
    (McIlwraith)
78 S.D. supplied by Q4.
79 *tongue and belly:* tongue and entrails were left for the gods in
    ancient sacrifices (Lucas)
81 *throughly* thoroughly

You have heard it rumour'd for these many years,
None of our family dies, but there is seen
The shape of an old woman, which is given          90
By tradition, to us, to have been murther'd
By her nephews, for her riches. Such a figure
One night, as the Prince sat up late at's book,
Appear'd to him; when crying out for help,
The gentlemen of's chamber found his Grace          95
All on a cold sweat, alter'd much in face
And language. Since which apparition
He hath grown worse and worse, and I much fear
He cannot live.
    *Bosola.* Sir, I would speak with you.
    *Pescara.*            We'll leave your Grace,          100
Wishing to the sick Prince, our noble lord,
All health of mind and body.
    *Cardinal.*         You are most welcome.
    [*Exeunt* PESCARA, MALATESTE *and* DOCTOR.]
[*aside*] Are you come? So: this fellow must not know
By any means I had intelligence
In our Duchess' death. For, though I counsell'd it,          105
The full of all the'engagement seem'd to grow
From Ferdinand. Now sir, how fares our sister?
I do not think but sorrow makes her look
Like to an oft-dy'd garment. She shall now
Taste comfort from me: why do you look so wildly?          110
Oh, the fortune of your master here, the Prince
Dejects you, but be you of happy comfort:
If you'll do one thing for me I'll entreat,
Though he had a cold tombstone o'er his bones,
I'll'd make you what you would be.
    *Bosola.*         Any thing;          115
Give it me in a breath, and let me fly to't:
They that think long, small expedition win,
For musing much o'th' end, cannot begin.          [*Enter* JULIA.]
    *Julia.* Sir, will you come in to supper?
    *Cardinal.*        I am busy, leave me.
    *Julia* [*aside*]. What an excellent shape hath that fellow!          120
                         *Exit.*

106 *The full of all th'engagement* Q1 (Q2, Q3, Q4 . . . th'agreement)
     the complete scope of Bosola's engagement to act
     as intelligencer
115 *you would be* Q1 (Q2, Q3 you should be; Q4 you'd be)
116 *it me* Q1, Q4 (Q2, Q3 me it)

*Cardinal.* 'Tis thus: Antonio lurks here in Milan;
Inquire him out, and kill him: while he lives
Our sister cannot marry, and I have thought
Of an excellent match for her: do this, and style me
Thy advancement.

125    *Bosola.*           But by what means shall I find him out?
      *Cardinal.* There is a gentleman, call'd Delio
Here in the camp, that hath been long approv'd
His loyal friend. Set eye upon that fellow,
Follow him to mass; may be Antonio,

130 Although he do account religion
But a school-name, for fashion of the world,
May accompany him: or else go inquire out
Delio's confessor, and see if you can bribe
Him to reveal it: there are a thousand ways

135 A man might find to trace him: as, to know
What fellows haunt the Jews for taking up
Great sums of money, for sure he's in want;
Or else go to th' picture-makers, and learn
Who brought her picture lately: some of these
Happily may take—

140    *Bosola.*           Well, I'll not freeze i'th' business,
I would see that wretched thing, Antonio,
Above all sights i'th' world.
     *Cardinal.*          Do, and be happy.      *Exit.*
     *Bosola.* This fellow doth breed basalisks in's eyes,
He's nothing else but murder: yet he seems

145 Not to have notice of the Duchess' death.
'Tis his cunning: I must follow his example;
There cannot be a surer way to trace,
Than that of an old fox.     [*Enter* JULIA *with a pistol.*]
     *Julia.*           So, sir, you are well met.
     *Bosola.* How now?
     *Julia.*           Nay, the doors are fast enough.

150 Now sir, I will make you confess your treachery.
     *Bosola.* Treachery?
     *Julia.*           Yes, confess to me
Which of my women 'twas you hir'd, to put
Love-powder into my drink?
     *Bosola.*            Love-powder?

---

125 *But by* Q1 (Q2, Q3, Q4 By)
127 *Here in the camp:* cf. III, iii, 1–16; *approv'd* proved, confirmed
139 *brought* Q1, Q2, Q3 (Q4 [omits]): see Textual Appendix—A.
140 *Happily* haply

*Julia.* Yes, when I was at Malfi;
Why should I fall in love with such a face else?                    155
I have already suffer'd for thee so much pain,
The only remedy to do me good
Is to kill my longing.
    *Bosola.*            Sure, your pistol holds
Nothing but perfumes or kissing-comfits: excellent lady,
You have a pretty way on't to discover                             160
Your longing. Come, come, I'll disarm you
And arm you thus: [*embraces her*] yet this is wondrous
                                            strange.
    *Julia.* Compare thy form and my eyes together,
You'll find my love no such great miracle.
[*Kisses him*]. Now you'll say                                     165
I am a wanton. This nice modesty in ladies
Is but a troublesome familiar
That haunts them.
    *Bosola.* Know you me, I am a blunt soldier.
    *Julia.*                         The better:
Sure, there wants fire where there are no lively sparks            170
Of roughness.
    *Bosola.*      And I want compliment.
    *Julia.*                      Why, ignorance
In courtship cannot make you do amiss,
If you have a heart to do well.
    *Bosola.*                  You are very fair.
    *Julia.* Nay, if you lay beauty to my charge,
I must plead unguilty.
    *Bosola.*              Your bright eyes                         175
Carry a quiver of darts in them, sharper
Than sunbeams.
    *Julia.*        You will mar me with commendation,
Put yourself to the charge of courting me,
Whereas now I woo you.
    *Bosola* [*aside*]. I have it, I will work upon this creature,  180
Let us grow most amorously familiar.
If the great Cardinal now should see me thus,
Would he not count me a villain?
    *Julia.* No, he might count me a wanton,
Not lay a scruple of offence on you:                               185

159 *kissing-comfits* comfits used to sweeten the breath (*cf.* modern
       cachous)
167 *familiar* familiar spirit
171 *want compliment* am lacking in complimentary language
179 *woo* ed. (Q1, Q2, Q4 woe; Q3 wo)

For if I see, and steal a diamond,
The fault is not i'th' stone, but in me the thief
That purloins it. I am sudden with you;
We that are great women of pleasure, use to cut off
190    These uncertain wishes and unquiet longings,
And in an instant join the sweet delight
And the pretty excuse together: had you been i'th' street,
Under my chamber window, even there
I should have courted you.
  *Bosola.*     Oh, you are an excellent lady.
195    *Julia.* Bid me do somewhat for you presently
To express I love you.
  *Bosola.*    I will, and if you love me,
Fail not to effect it.
The Cardinal is grown wondrous melancholy,
Demand the cause, let him not put you off
200    With feign'd excuse; discover the main ground on't.
  *Julia.* Why would you know this?
  *Bosola.*     I have depended on him,
And I hear that he is fall'n in some disgrace
With the Emperor: if he be, like the mice
That forsake falling houses, I would shift
205    To other dependence.
  *Julia.* You shall not need follow the wars:
I'll be your maintenance.
  *Bosola.* And I your loyal servant;
But I cannot leave my calling.
  *Julia.*     Not leave an
210    Ungrateful general for the love of a sweet lady?
You are like some, cannot sleep in feather-beds,
But must have blocks for their pillows.
  *Bosola.*     Will you do this?
  *Julia.* Cunningly.
  *Bosola.*   Tomorrow I'll expect th'intelligence.
  *Julia.* Tomorrow? get you into my cabinet;
215    You shall have it with you: do not delay me,
No more than I do you. I am like one
That is condemn'd: I have my pardon promis'd,
But I would see it seal'd. Go, get you in,
You shall see me wind my tongue about his heart

185    *scruple* a minute quantity
193: Q1 (Q2, Q3, Q4 [omit])
195    *presently* immediately
206    *shall not need* Q1, Q2, Q4 (Q3 shall need)
209    *my calling* Q1, Q2, Q4 (Q3 your calling)

Like a skein of silk.                                                    220
[BOSOLA *withdraws behind the traverse; enter* CARDINAL.]
   *Cardinal.* Where are you?    [*Enter* SERVANTS]
   *Servants.*                    Here.
   *Cardinal.*                   Let none upon your lives
Have conference with the Prince Ferdinand,
Unless I know it. [*aside*] In this distraction
He may reveal the murther.            [*Exeunt* SERVANTS.]
Yond's my ling'ring consumption:                                         225
I am weary of her; and by any means
Would be quit of—
   *Julia.*          How now, my Lord?
What ails you?
   *Cardinal.* Nothing.
   *Julia.*                   Oh, you are much alter'd:
Come, I must be your secretary, and remove
This lead from off your bosom; what's the matter?                         230
   *Cardinal.* I may not tell you.
   *Julia.*                    Are you so far in love with sorrow,
You cannot part with part of it? or think you
I cannot love your Grace when you are sad,
As well as merry? or do you suspect
I, that have been a secret to your heart                                  235
These many winters, cannot be the same
Unto your tongue?
   *Cardinal.*          Satisfy thy longing.
The only way to make thee keep my counsel
Is not to tell thee.
   *Julia.*            Tell your echo this,
Or flatterers, that, like echoes, still report                            240
What they hear, though most imperfect, and not me:
For, if that you be true unto yourself,
I'll know.
   *Cardinal.* Will you rack me?
   *Julia.*                    No, judgment shall
Draw it from you. It is an equal fault,
To tell one's secrets unto all, or none.                                  245
   *Cardinal.* The first argues folly.
   *Julia.*                    But the last tyranny.

227 *Would be quit of*— ed. (Q1, Q2 quit off; Q3, Q4 quit off her;
    Dyce, Hazlitt, Vaughan, McIlwraith: quit of; Lucas,
    with Sampson, retains Q1 reading but suggests that
    'quite off' may be possible).
229 *secretary* confidant

 *Cardinal.* Very well; why, imagine I have committed
Some secret deed which I desire the world
May never hear of!
 *Julia.*     Therefore may not I know it?
250 You have conceal'd for me as great a sin
As adultery. Sir, never was occasion
For perfect trial of my constancy
Till now. Sir, I beseech you.
 *Cardinal.*    You'll repent it.
 *Julia.*        Never.
 *Cardinal.* It hurries thee to ruin: I'll not tell thee.
255 Be well advis'd, and think what danger 'tis
To receive a prince's secrets: they that do,
Had need have their breasts hoop'd with adamant
To contain them. I pray thee yet be satisfi'd,
Examine thine own frailty; 'tis more easy
260 To tie knots, than unloose them: 'tis a secret
That, like a ling'ring poison, may chance lie
Spread in thy veins, and kill thee seven year hence.
 *Julia.* Now you dally with me.
 *Cardinal.*    No more; thou shalt know it.
By my appointment the great Duchess of Malfi
265 And two of her young children, four nights since
Were strangled.
 *Julia.*  Oh Heaven! Sir, what have you done?
 *Cardinal.* How now? how settles this? Think you your
          bosom

Will be a grave dark and obscure enough
For such a secret?
 *Julia.*  You have undone yourself, sir.
 *Cardinal.* Why?
 *Julia.*  It lies not in me to conceal it.
270  *Cardinal.*      No?
Come, I will swear you to't upon this book.
 *Julia.* Most religiously.
 *Cardinal.*  Kiss it.  [*She kisses a Bible.*]
Now you shall never utter it; thy curiosity
Hath undone thee; thou'rt poison'd with that book.
275 Because I knew thou couldst not keep my counsel,
I have bound thee to't by death.  [*Enter* BOSOLA]

251 *Sir, never was occasion* Q1 (Q2, Q3, Q4 Sir, I beseech you)
267 *how settles this?* 'A figure drawn from the settling of liquid,
 hence its clarifying; as if the Cardinal now saw the situa-
 tion more clearly.' (Sampson)

*Bosola.* For pity-sake, hold.
*Cardinal.*                    Ha, Bosola!
*Julia.*                          I forgive you
This equal piece of justice you have done:
For I betray'd your counsel to that fellow;
He overheard it; that was the cause I said        280
It lay not in me to conceal it.
*Bosola.*                 Oh foolish woman,
Couldst not thou have poison'd him?
*Julia.*                        'Tis weakness,
Too much to think what should have been done. I go,
I know not whither.                        [*Dies.*]
*Cardinal.*        Wherefore com'st thou hither?
*Bosola.* That I might find a great man, like yourself,   285
Not out of his wits, as the Lord Ferdinand,
To remember my service.
*Cardinal.*                I'll have thee hew'd in pieces.
*Bosola.* Make not yourself such a promise of that life
Which is not yours to dispose of.
*Cardinal.*                Who plac'd thee here?
*Bosola.* Her lust, as she intended.
*Cardinal.*                Very well;            290
Now you know me for your fellow murderer.
*Bosola.* And wherefore should you lay fair marble colours
Upon your rotten purposes to me?
Unless you imitate some that do plot great treasons,
And when they have done, go hide themselves i'th' graves   295
Of those were actors in't.
*Cardinal.* No more: there is a fortune attends thee.
*Bosola.* Shall I go sue to Fortune any longer?
'Tis the fool's pilgrimage.
*Cardinal.*                I have honours in store for thee.
*Bosola.* There are a many ways that conduct to seeming   300
Honour, and some of them very dirty ones.
*Cardinal.* Throw to the devil
Thy melancholy; the fire burns well,
What need we keep a stirring of't, and make
A greater smother? Thou wilt kill Antonio?       305
*Bosola.*   Yes.
*Cardinal.*    Take up that body.

292–3: i.e. why give the crumbling and corrupt fabric of your
       purposes the appearance of marble's strength and beauty?
298  *to Fortune* ed. (Q1 to fortune, Q2, Q3, a fortune; Q4 a Fortune)
300  *a many ways* Q1 (Q2, Q3, Q4 many ways)
305  *greater* Q1 (Q2, Q3, Q4 great)

*Bosola.*                              I think I shall
Shortly grow the common bier for churchyards!
*Cardinal.* I will allow thee some dozen of attendants,
To aid thee in the murther.
310  *Bosola.* Oh, by no means: physicians that apply horse-
leeches to any rank swelling, use to cut off their tails, that
the blood may run through them the faster. Let me have no
train, when I go to shed blood, lest it make me have a greater,
when I ride to the gallows.
*Cardinal.* Come to me after midnight, to help to remove
315                                                that body
To her own lodging. I'll give out she di'd o'th' plague;
'Twill breed the less inquiry after her death.
*Bosola.* Where's Castruchio her husband?
*Cardinal.* He's rode to Naples to take possession
320  Of Antonio's citadel.
*Bosola.* Believe me, you have done a very happy turn.
*Cardinal.* Fail not to come. There is the master-key
Of our lodgings: and by that you may conceive
What trust I plant in you.                    *Exit.*
*Bosola.*              You shall find me ready.
325  Oh poor Antonio, though nothing be so needful
To thy estate, as pity, yet I find
Nothing so dangerous. I must look to my footing;
In such slippery ice-pavements men had need
To be frost-nail'd well: they may break their necks else.
330  The president's here afore me: how this man
Bears up in blood! seems fearless! Why, 'tis well:
Security some men call the suburbs of hell,
Only a dead wall between. Well, good Antonio,
I'll seek thee out; and all my care shall be
335  To put thee into safety from the reach
Of these most cruel biters, that have got
Some of thy blood already. It may be,
I'll join with thee in a most just revenge.
The weakest arm is strong enough, that strikes
340  With the sword of justice. Still methinks the Duchess
Haunts me: there, there: 'tis nothing but my melancholy.
O penitence, let me truly taste thy cup,
That throws men down, only to raise them up.      *Exit.*

307 *bier* Q3, Q4 (Q1, Q2 beare)
330 *president* precedent
331 *bears up in blood* keeps up his courage (Lucas)
332 *security* freedom from anxiety; carelessness
336 *biters* sheep-biters *cf.* V,ii, 51 n.
343 *raise* Q1, Q3, Q4 (Q2 rise)

## Scene iii

[*Enter* ANTONIO *and* DELIO; *there is an*] ECHO (*from the* DUCHESS' *grave*).

*Delio.* Yond's the Cardinal's window. This fortification
Grew from the ruins of an ancient abbey:
And to yond side o'th' river lies a wall,
Piece of a cloister, which in my opinion
Gives the best echo that you ever heard;                          5
So hollow, and so dismal, and withal
So plain in the distinction of our words,
That many have suppos'd it is a spirit
That answers.
    *Antonio.*     I do love these ancient ruins:
We never tread upon them, but we set                             10
Our foot upon some reverend history,
And, questionless, here in this open court,
Which now lies naked to the injuries
Of stormy weather, some men lie interr'd
Lov'd the church so well, and gave so largely to't,             15
They thought it should have canopi'd their bones
Till doomsday. But all things have their end:
Churches and cities, which have diseases like to men
Must have like death that we have.
    *Echo.*                         *Like death that we have.*
    *Delio.* Now the echo hath caught you.
    *Antonio.*                 It groan'd, methought, and gave     20
A very deadly accent!
    *Echo.*                 *Deadly accent.*
    *Delio.* I told you 'twas a pretty one. You may make it
A huntsman, or a falconer, a musician
Or a thing of sorrow.
    *Echo.*             *A thing of sorrow.*
    *Antonio.* Ay sure: that suits it best.
    *Echo.*                     *That suits it best.*               25
    *Antonio.* 'Tis very like my wife's voice.
    *Echo.*                         *Ay, wife's voice.*
    *Delio.* Come: let's walk farther from't:

14 *some men lie* ed. (Q1 some men lye; Q2, Q3 some lye; Q4 Some
    lie)
27 *let's* Q4 (Q1, Q2, Q3 let's us)

I would not have you go to th' Cardinal's tonight:
Do not.
    *Echo. Do not.*
30    *Delio.* Wisdom doth not more moderate wasting sorrow
Than time: take time for't: be mindful of thy safety.
    *Echo. Be mindful of thy safety.*
    *Antonio.*                    Necessity compels me:
Make scrutiny throughout the passages
Of your own life; you'll find it impossible
To fly your fate.
35    *Echo. O fly your fate.*
    *Delio.* Hark: the dead stones seem to have pity on you
And give you good counsel.
    *Antonio.*             Echo, I will not talk with thee;
For thou art a dead thing.
    *Echo.*             *Thou art a dead thing.*
    *Antonio.* My Duchess is asleep now,
40    And her little ones, I hope sweetly: oh Heaven
Shall I never see her more?
    *Echo.*             *Never see her more.*
    *Antonio.* I mark'd not one repetition of the Echo
But that: and on the sudden, a clear light
Presented me a face folded in sorrow.
    *Delio.* Your fancy; merely.
45    *Antonio.*             Come: I'll be out of this ague;
For to live thus, is not indeed to live:
It is a mockery, and abuse of life.
I will not henceforth save myself by halves;
Lose all, or nothing.
    *Delio.*         Your own virtue save you.
50    I'll fetch your eldest son; and second you:
It may be that the sight of his own blood
Spread in so sweet a figure, may beget
The more compassion.
    *Antonio.*        However, fare you well.
Though in our miseries Fortune hath a part
55    Yet, in our noble sufferings, she hath none:
Contempt of pain, that we may call our own.
                                    *Exe[unt].*

28 *you go to* Q1b, Q4 (Q1a you too to; Q2, Q3, you to)
33 *passages* Q4 (Q1, Q2, Q3 passes)
35 speech-prefix: Q4 *Ecc.* (Q1, Q2, Q3 [omit])
40–1 See Critical Notes on III,v, 79–80.
47 *a mockery* Q1, Q2 (Q3, Q4 mockery)
52 *spread in* Q1 (Q2, Q3, Q4 spread into)
53 *Antonio* ed. see Textual Appendix—A.

### Scene iv

[*Enter*] CARDINAL, PESCARA, MALATESTE, RODERIGO, GRISOLAN.

*Cardinal.* You shall not watch tonight by the sick Prince;
His Grace is very well recover'd.
*Malateste.* Good my lord, suffer us.
*Cardinal.*                    Oh, by no means:
The noise and change of object in his eye
Doth more distract him. I pray, all to bed,                    5
And though you hear him in his violent fit,
Do not rise, I entreat you.
*Pescara.*                    So sir, we shall not—
*Cardinal.* Nay, I must have you promise
Upon your honours, for I was enjoin'd to't
By himself; and he seem'd to urge it sensibly.                 10
*Pescara.* Let our honours bind this trifle.
*Cardinal.* Nor any of your followers.
*Pescara.*                         Neither.
*Cardinal.* It may be to make trial of your promise
When he's asleep, myself will rise, and feign
Some of his mad tricks, and cry out for help,                  15
And feign myself in danger.
*Malateste.*                  If your throat were cutting,
I'll'd not come at you, now I have protested against it.
*Cardinal.* Why, I thank you.              [*Withdraws.*]
*Grisolan.*                    'Twas a foul storm tonight.
*Roderigo.* The Lord Ferdinand's chamber shook like an
                                                     osier.
*Malateste.* 'Twas nothing but pure kindness in the devil,     20
To rock his own child.              *Exeunt* [RODERIGO,
                         MALATESTE, PESCARA, GRISOLAN.]
*Cardinal.* The reason why I would not suffer these
About my brother, is because at midnight
I may with better privacy convey
Julia's body to her own lodging. O, my conscience!            25
I would pray now: but the devil takes away my heart
For having any confidence in prayer.
About this hour I appointed Bosola
To fetch the body: when he hath serv'd my turn,
He dies.                                                       30

                         *Exit.* [*Enter* BOSOLA.]

*Bosola.* Ha! 'twas the Cardinal's voice. I heard him name
Bosola, and my death: listen, I hear one's footing.

[*Enter* FERDINAND.]

*Ferdinand.* Strangling is a very quiet death.
*Bosola.* Nay then I see, I must stand upon my guard.
*Ferdinand.* What say' to that? Whisper, softly: do you
35                                         agree to't?
So it must be done i'th' dark: the Cardinal
Would not for a thousand pounds the doctor should see it.
                                                *Exit.*
*Bosola.* My death is plotted; here's the consequence of
                                                murther.
*We value not desert, nor Christian breath,*
40    *When we know black deeds must be cur'd with death.*

[*Withdraws. Enter* ANTONIO *and a* SERVANT.]

*Servant.* Here stay sir, and be confident, I pray:
I'll fetch you a dark lanthorn.                  *Exit.*
*Antonio.*                 Could I take him
At his prayers, there were hope of pardon.
*Bosola.* Fall right my sword: [*strikes* ANTONIO *down from
                                                behind.*]
45    I'll not give thee so much leisure as to pray.
*Antonio.* Oh, I am gone. Thou hast ended a long suit,
In a minute.
*Bosola.*    What art thou?
*Antonio.*                 A most wretched thing
That only have thy benefit in death,
To appear myself.    [*Enter* SERVANT *with a dark lanthorn.*]
*Servant.*         Where are you sir?
*Antonio.* Very near my home. Bosola?
50    *Servant.*                         Oh misfortune!
*Bosola* [*to* SERVANT]. Smother thy pity, thou art dead else.
                                                Antonio!
The man I would have sav'd 'bove mine own life!
We are merely the stars' tennis-balls, struck and banded
Which way please them: oh good Antonio,
55    I'll whisper one thing in thy dying ear,
Shall make thy heart break quickly. Thy fair Duchess
And two sweet children—

35 *what say'* Q1, Q2 (Q3, Q4 what say you)
53 *banded* bandied

*Antonio.*                    Their very names
Kindle a little life in me.
*Bosola.*                 Are murder'd!
*Antonio.* Some men have wish's to die
At the hearing of sad tidings: I am glad                      60
That I shall do't in sadness: I would not now
Wish my wounds balm'd, nor heal'd: for I have no use
To put my life to. In all our quest of greatness,
Like wanton boys, whose pastime is their care,
We follow after bubbles, blown in th'air.                     65
Pleasure of life, what is't? only the good hours
Of an ague: merely a preparative to rest,
To endure vexation. I do not ask
The process of my death: only commend me
To Delio.
*Bosola.* Break, heart!                                       70
*Antonio.* And let my son fly the courts of princes. [*Dies.*]
*Bosola.* Thou seem'st to have lov'd Antonio?
*Servant.*                 I brought him hither,
To have reconcil'd him to the Cardinal.
*Bosola.* I do not ask thee that.
Take him up, if thou tender thine own life,                   75
And bear him where the Lady Julia
Was wont to lodge. Oh, my fate moves swift.
I have this Cardinal in the forge already,
Now I'll bring him to th' hammer. (O direful misprision!)
I will not imitate things glorious,                           80
No more than base: I'll be mine own example.
On, on: and look thou represent, for silence,
The thing thou bear'st.
                                        *Exeunt.*

60 *sad tidings:* see Textual Appendix—A.   61 *sadness* seriousness
65 *in th' air* Q1 (Q2, Q3, Q4 i'th' air)
73 *to the Cardinal* Q1 (Q2, Q3, Q4 with the Cardinal)
74 *ask thee* want thee to do             75 *tender* care for
79 *misprision* mistake

## Scene v

*[Enter]* CARDINAL (*with a book*).

*Cardinal.* I am puzzl'd in a question about hell:
He says, in hell there's one material fire,
And yet it shall not burn all men alike.
Lay him by. How tedious is a guilty conscience!
5  When I look into the fishponds, in my garden,
Methinks I see a thing arm'd with a rake
That seems to strike at me. Now? Art thou come?

*[Enter* BOSOLA *and* SERVANT *with* ANTONIO'S *body.*]

Thou look'st ghastly:
There sits in thy face some great determination,
Mix'd with some fear.
10  *Bosola.*              Thus it lightens into action:
I am come to kill thee.
   *Cardinal.*              Ha? Help! our guard!
   *Bosola.* Thou art deceiv'd:
They are out of thy howling.
   *Cardinal.* Hold: and I will faithfully divide
Revenues with thee.
15  *Bosola.*              Thy prayers and proffers
Are both unseasonable.
   *Cardinal.*              Raise the watch:
We are betray'd!
   *Bosola.*        I have confin'd your flight:
I'll suffer your retreat to Julia's chamber,
But no further.
   *Cardinal.*     Help: we are betray'd!

*[Enter* PESCARA, MALATESTE, RODERIGO *and* GRISOLAN, *above.*]

*Malateste.*                    Listen.
*Cardinal.* My dukedom for rescue!
20  *Roderigo.*                Fie upon his counterfeiting.
*Malateste.* Why, 'tis not the Cardinal.
   *Roderigo.*                    Yes, yes, 'tis he:
But I'll see him hang'd, ere I'll go down to him.
   *Cardinal.* Here's a plot upon me; I am assaulted. I am
                                                     lost,

10 *lightens* flashes out into
14 *Hold: and I* Q1 (Q2, Q3, Q4 Hold: I)

Unless some rescue!
  *Grisolan.*          He doth this pretty well:
But it will not serve to laugh me out of mine honour.    25
  *Cardinal.* The sword's at my throat!
  *Roderigo.*         You would not bawl so loud then.
  *Malateste.* Come, come: let's go to bed: he told us thus
                         much aforehand.
  *Pescara.* He wish'd you should not come at him: but
                         believ't,
The accent of the voice sounds not in jest.
I'll down to him, howsoever, and with engines    30
Force ope the doors.                *[Exit.]*
  *Roderigo.*      Let's follow him aloof,
And note how the Cardinal will laugh at him.
                      *[Exeunt above.]*
  *Bosola.* There's for you first:
'Cause you shall not unbarricade the door
To let in rescue.          *He kills the* SERVANT.    35
  *Cardinal.* What cause hast thou to pursue my life?
  *Bosola.*                Look there.
  *Cardinal.* Antonio!
  *Bosola.*        Slain by my hand unwittingly.
Pray, and be sudden: when thou kill'd'st thy sister,
Thou took'st from Justice her most equal balance,
And left her naught but her sword.
  *Cardinal.*            O mercy!    40
  *Bosola.* Now it seems thy greatness was only outward:
For thou fall'st faster of thyself than calamity
Can drive thee. I'll not waste longer time. There.
                 *[Stabs the* CARDINAL.]
  *Cardinal.* Thou hast hurt me.
  *Bosola.*            Again. *[Stabs him again.]*
  *Cardinal.*         Shall I die like a leveret
Without any resistance? Help, help, help!    45
I am slain.             *[Enter* FERDINAND.]
  *Ferdinand.* Th'alarum? give me a fresh horse.
Rally the vaunt-guard; or the day is lost.
Yield, yield! I give you the honour of arms,
Shake my sword over you, will you yield?
  *Cardinal.* Help me, I am your brother.

27 *let's* Q2, Q3, Q4 (Q1 lets's)     30 *engines* tools, instruments
40 *her sword* Q1 (Q2, Q3, Q4 the sword)
47 *vaunt-guard* vanguard
48 *the honour of arms*;  52 *There flies your ransome*: see Critical
    Notes.

50      *Ferdinand.*                    The devil?
    My brother fight upon the adverse party?
    (*He wounds the* CARDINAL *and, in the scuffle, gives* BOSOLA
    *his death wound.*)
    There flies your ransome.
    *Cardinal.*               Oh Justice:
    I suffer now for what hath former bin
    *Sorrow is held the eldest child of sin.*
55      *Ferdinand.* Now you're brave fellows. Caesar's fortune
    was harder than Pompey's: Caesar died in the arms of
    prosperity, Pompey at the feet of disgrace: you both
    died in the field, the pain's nothing. Pain many times is
    taken away with the apprehension of greater, as the tooth-
60      ache with the sight of a barber that comes to pull it out:
    there's philosophy for you.
    *Bosola.* Now my revenge is perfect: sink, thou main cause
    Of my undoing: the last part of my life
    Hath done me best service.          *He kills* FERDINAND.
65      *Ferdinand.* Give me some wet hay, I am broken winded.
    I do account this world but a dog-kennel:
    I will vault credit, and affect high pleasures
    Beyond death.
    *Bosola.*      He seems to come to himself,
    Now he's so near the bottom.
70      *Ferdinand.* My sister, oh! my sister, there's the cause on't.
    *Whether we fall by ambition, blood, or lust,*
    *Like diamonds we are cut with our own dust.*          [*Dies.*]
    *Cardinal.* Thou hast thy payment too.
    *Bosola.* Yes, I hold my weary soul in my teeth;
75      'Tis ready to part from me. I do glory
    That thou, which stood'st like a huge pyramid
    Begun upon a large and ample base,
    Shalt end in a little point, a kind of nothing.

    [*Enter* PESCARA, MALATESTE, RODERIGO *and* GRISOLAN.]

    *Pescara.* How now, my lord?
    *Malateste.*              O sad disaster!
    *Roderigo.*                          How comes this?
80      *Bosola.* Revenge, for the Duchess of Malfi, murdered
    By th' Aragonian brethren; for Antonio,
    Slain by this hand; for lustful Julia,

50 *The devil?* Qq, Lucas (Dyce, Hazlitt, Sampson, McIlwraith:
    The devil!)
51 *My brother* Q1, Q2 (Q3, Q4 My brothers)          53 *bin* been
68 *Beyond death* Q1 (Q2, Q3, Q4 [omit])
82 *this hand* Q4 (Q1, Q2, Q3 his hand)

Poison'd by this man; and lastly, for myself,
That was an actor in the main of all,
Much 'gainst mine own good nature, yet i'th' end          85
Neglected.
   *Pescara.* How now, my lord?
   *Cardinal.*             Look to my brother:
He gave us these large wounds, as we were struggling
Here i'th'rushes. And now, I pray, let me
Be laid by, and never thought of.       [*Dies.*]
   *Pescara.* How fatally, it seems, he did withstand          90
His own rescue!
   *Malateste.*       Thou wretched thing of blood,
How came Antonio by his death?
   *Bosola.* In a mist: I know not how;
Such a mistake as I have often seen
In a play. Oh, I am gone:          95
We are only like dead walls, or vaulted graves
That, ruin'd, yields no echo. Fare you well;
It may be pain: but no harm to me to die
In so good a quarrel. Oh this gloomy world,
In what a shadow, or deep pit of darkness          100
Doth, womanish, and fearful, mankind live?
Let worthy minds ne'er stagger in distrust
To suffer death or shame for what is just:
Mine is another voyage.         [*Dies.*]
   *Pescara.* The noble Delio, as I came to th'palace,          105
Told me of Antonio's being here, and show'd me
A pretty gentleman his son and heir.
[*Enter* DELIO *with* ANTONIO'S *son.*]
   *Malateste.* O sir, you come too late.
   *Delio.*                I heard so, and
Was arm'd for't ere I came. Let us make noble use
Of this great ruin; and join all our force          110
To establish this young hopeful gentleman
In's mother's right. These wretched eminent things
Leave no more fame behind 'em, than should one
Fall in a frost, and leave his print in snow,
As soon as the sun shines, it ever melts          115
Both form and matter. I have ever thought
Nature doth nothing so great for great men,
As when she's pleas'd to make them lords of truth:
*Integrity of life is fame's best friend,*
*Which nobly, beyond death, shall crown the end.*   *Exeunt.*          120

*FINIS.*

# CRITICAL NOTES

**1** *priuatly, at the Black-Friers; and publiquely at the Globe,*
i.e. the play was performed in a private as well as in a
public theatre. For discussion of the differences in
dramatic material, presentation and audiences of the
public and private theatres, see Alfred Harbage, *Shakespeare and the Rival Traditions* (New York, 1952) and
William A. Armstrong, 'The Audience of the Elizabethan
Private Theatres', *Review of English Studies* N.S. X
(1959), 234–49.

*The perfect and exact copy:* not a claim to be taken
literally. See J. R. Brown, 'The Printing of John
Webster's Plays (I)', *Studies in Bibliography* VI (1954),
117–40 [especially 128–9].

**3** *[Dramatis Personæ]* Qq simply provide the names of the
actors. Q1 and Q2 have the same list which is unique in
printed drama of the sixteenth and seventeenth centuries
in giving two casts, thus indicating that there were at
least two different productions before 1623. Q3 lists the
cast of the Restoration production first performed by the
Duke's Company in 1664 with Betterton as Bosola and
Mrs. Betterton as the Duchess. This production filled
the theatre for eight days successively and proved one
of the company's best stock tragedies. The only major
change in the 1664 cast apparent in the 1678 list is in
the part of Julia. Q4 contains the cast list for the
abbreviated and altered version of the play as it was
presented on 22 July, 1707, at the Queen's Theatre in
the Haymarket with Verbruggen as Ferdinand and Keene
as the Cardinal.

The first list, of Q1 and Q2, names the parts briefly and
omits Castruchio, Roderigo, Grisolan and Old Lady. Q4
is the first to distinguish four of the madmen, though the
mad priest is incorrectly labelled as a mad parson (see
p. 112 below). Forobosco's, not a speaking part, is
omitted from the lists of Q3 and Q4. In the first list it is
assigned to N. Towley; but as no actor's name is given
for Malateste, this may be a mistake. Dr. Brown has
suggested (*op. cit.*, p. 133) that since R. Pallant, whose
name appears in this list, only joined the King's Men in
1619–20, Forobosco may have had a speech which was

inserted in performances about that time. In the play he
is named as keeper of the key of the park gate. Perhaps
he was the chief court officer, distinguished from the
others by some item of uniform.

CASTRUCHIO: F. L. Lucas (*Webster*, ii, 132) notes that
Castruchio's name is derived from the historic Petrucci,
Cardinal of Siena, in Bandello whose name Belleforest,
followed by Painter, changes to Castruccio. But in
Painter the name still belongs to 'Castruccio, the Cardinal
of Siena'. The reason for Webster's adoption of the name
for the fictitious character of Julia's old husband is surely
that it *sounds* as if it meant 'castrated' and, therefore,
implies the connotations given in Florio's gloss of
*Castrone*—'a gelded man. . . . Also a noddie, a meacocke,
[effeminate person] a cuckold, a ninnie, a gull.': all of
which suit the stage character of Old Castruchio.

CARIOLA: Since Florio glosses *Carriolo* or *Carriuola* as,
among other things, a 'trundle-bed' Webster's choice of
the name was appropriate 'in an age when personal
servants slept in trundle-beds close to their employers'
beds'. See G. K. Hunter, 'Notes on Webster's Tragedies',
*Notes and Queries* N.S. IV (1957), p. 55.

4    *George Harding*, thirteenth Baron Berkeley, though only
twenty-two when Webster dedicated the first quarto to
him, was known as a good friend of the theatre in general
and of the King's Men in particular.

5–6  *Commendatory Verses* by Thomas Middleton, William
Rowley and John Ford: each of these dramatists was at
one time a collaborator with Webster.

7    *Act I, Scene i.* The action, up to the end of II, iii, takes
place in the Duchess' palace at Amalfi.

8    I, i, 58–65. To uses of 'geometry' in Bosola's sense here that
have been noted by F. L. Lucas, R. W. Dent adds one
from Melbancke's *Philotimus* (1583) where it implies stiff
props (in this case those of the human skeleton). The
frontispiece of Gabriele Baldini's *John Webster e il
linguaggio della tragedia* illustrates Bosola's meaning from
Peter Breughel's representation of cripples. See R.
W. Dent, *John Webster's Borrowing* (Berkeley and Los
Angeles, 1960), pp. 179–80; Gabriele Baldini, *John
Webster e il linguaggio della tragedia* (Rome, 1953),
frontispiece and p. 160; also Clifford Leech, *Webster:
'The Duchess of Malfi'* (1963), pp. 43–4.

10   I, ii, 30 *children of Ismael.* According to *N.E.D.* the name
Ismaelite was formerly given (especially by the Jews) to

the Arabs as descendants of Ishmael, Abraham's son by the bondwoman Hagar. (See Genesis xvi, 15–16; xvii, 18–27; xxi, 9–21; xxv, 12–18, and I Chronicles i, 29–30.) If the reading 'children of Ismael' is correct, Julia's pun refers simply to the Arabs as tent-dwellers. Despite this obvious meaning I suspect that we should read 'children of Israel'.

First, the spelling 'Ismael' was decidedly old-fashioned for a play printed in 1623. It was to be found in early sixteenth-century versions of the Bible such as Coverdale's (1535), 'Matthew's Bible' (1537) and Cranmer's (1540), and it was used in the Bishops' Bible of 1568; but the spelling 'Ishmael' was introduced in the Genevan version of 1560 and this version, which was reprinted some two hundred times, was far the most popular in Elizabethan England. The same spelling was retained in the King James (or 'Authorized') Version of 1611.

Secondly, although it might have been known that, especially among the Jews, Arabs were referred to as the children of Ishmael, there is no reference in the Old Testament itself to Ishmael or his descendants as tent-dwellers. On the contrary, in Genesis xxv, 16 reference is made to their towns and castles and it was Jabal who, in Genesis iv, 20, was called 'the father of such as dwell in tents'. There are, however, several Old Testament references to the Israelites or children of Israel, both individually and collectively, dwelling in tents. Among these Psalm lxxviii, 55—'He cast out the heathen also before them, and made the tribes of Israel to dwell in their tents.'—and II Kings xiii, 5—'and the children of Israel dwelt in their tents, as aforetime.'— might be cited as obvious bases of Julia's pun. I suggest, therefore, that Webster originally wrote Israel which, by scribal or compositorial error became Ismael and thereby Julia's joke, though perfectly intelligible, lost some of its immediacy.

I, ii, 31–34: the double entendre here indicates a salacious trait in Ferdinand's mind.

I, ii, 38. Pliny's opinion was that in Portugal, along the River Tagus and about Lisbon, mares conceived from the west wind and brought forth foals as swift as the wind. See Holland's translation of Pliny's *Natural History* (1601) VIII, chapter 42, p. 222.

11   I, ii, 54–56. Just as ll. 31–34, reveal Ferdinand's understanding of Julia's nature as well as her wit, so these lines

demonstrate her jesting attitude to adultery and show
how her husband is duped by her jesting. *Cf.* II, iv, 3–5.

14   I, ii, 168–9. Bosola is referring to the story of the trans-
formation of Jupiter the Thunderer into a shower of gold
in order that he might reach Danae in her brazen tower.
*Cf.* II, ii, 18–20 and note on p. 108 below.

15   I, ii, 184–7. One is reminded here of Judas Iscariot.

16   I, ii, 210–12. P. Haworth, *English Hymns and Ballads and
other Studies in Popular Literature* (Oxford, 1927), pp.
116–17, relates this passage to Antonio's description of
the French court (I, i, 5–22) and concludes, 'Bosola's
speech seems therefore to express the moral purpose
Webster had in view in treating the story.'

I, ii, 219–20. In fact Laban's spotted sheep and cattle
became Jacob's. See Genesis xxx, 31–42, and *cf. The
Merchant of Venice* I, iii, 66–85.

18   I, ii, 280 ff. Clifford Leech, *Webster: 'The Duchess of Malfi'*,
p. 12, notes that 'we are now "in the gallery" where
Antonio was earlier told to see her: the locality has
changed without a break in the action'. It is also possible
that we are still in the Duchess' presence chamber, the
gallery being behind the traverse.

19   I, ii, 309. *St. Winifred*, a seventh-century Welsh saint,
(Gwenfrewi) had her head struck off by Caradoc ap
Alauc for rejecting his advances. St. Beuno, who was her
mother's brother, restored her to life, but from the place
where her head fell there issued the spring which gives
its name to Holywell, Flintshire. See also Textual
Appendix—A.

20   I, ii, 337–41. Just as the Duchess' words, with their
references to her will, a winding sheet and her husband's
tomb (I, ii, 294–300; 308–9; 370–1) foreshadow death,
these of Antonio adumbrate the horrors preceding her
death.

22   I, ii, 392. *Per verba de presenti*—'by words about the
present'. Martin W. Sampson first restored the *de*
omitted by Qq. Two articles, not always in agreement on
points of interpretation, which throw light on the
significance on these marriages and the contemporary
attitude to them are: D. P. Harding, 'Elizabethan Betro-
thals and *Measure for Measure*', *Journal of English and
Germanic Philology*, XLIX (1950), 139–58 and Ernest
Schanzer, 'The Marriage Contracts in *Measure for
Measure*', *Shakespeare Survey 13* (1960), 81–89. For
discussion of the significance of the Duchess' marriage to

her major-domo and the importance of this relationship in the play, see F. W. Wadsworth, 'Webster's *Duchess of Malfi* in the Light of Some Contemporary Ideas on Marriage and Remarriage', *Philological Quarterly*, XXXV (1956), 394–407; J. R. Mulryne, ' "The White Devil" and "The Duchess of Malfi" ', *Stratford-upon-Avon Studies 1: Jacobean Theatre* (1960), 201–25 [especially pp. 219–22]; Gunnar Boklund, *'The Duchess of Malfi' Sources, Themes, Characters* (Cambridge, Mass., 1962) pp. 95–97; Clifford Leech, *Webster: 'The Duchess of Malfi'*, pp. 50–57.

I, ii, 395. The Spheres, concentric, transparent hollow globes, were imagined by the older astronomers to revolve round the earth, carrying with them the heavenly bodies. Their motion was said to produce harmonious music.

23 I, ii, 413: *Alexander and Lodowick*. In the story referred to here, which, as F. L. Lucas indicates (*Webster*, ii, 142), is a version of 'one of the most famous stories of the Middle Ages, *Amis and Amiloun*' two friends are so alike that they change place without anyone noticing. When Lodowick marries the Princess of Hungaria in Alexander's name, he lays a naked sword between the Princess and himself each night so that his friend is not wronged.

24 II, i, 33–34. Bosola's imagery implies that the Old Lady is an old battle-ship getting ready for war on the high seas.

II, i, 42–43: i.e. 'when *you* are fasting and the offensiveness therefore at its worst'. (Lucas).

26 II, i, 101–2: *King Pippin*. The third of the three Carolingian monarchs of this name (*d.* 768) was the best known. His coronation, performed by St. Boniface, was a ceremony new to France. Among the important events of his reign were his expeditions to Italy in 754 and 756 which were made at the request of Pope Stephen II. By wresting the exarchate of Ravenna from Aistulf, King of the Lombards and conferring it on the Pope, Pippin III became the veritable creator of the papal state. Upon his death his kingdom was divided between his sons Charles (Charlemagne) and Carloman.

28 II, i, 168. *the midwife*, probably the Old Lady.

29 II, ii, 1–3. Bosola's lines could be soliloquy, with the Old Lady entering at 'breeding' as Dyce, Hazlitt and Vaughan indicate. Lucas makes the line an aside, with Bosola turning to the Old Lady at 'now?'. Sampson suggests that Bosola might be trying to gain information from her and with this I concur.

CRITICAL NOTES

II, ii, 6. *the glass-house*, i.e. the famous glass factory near the Blackfriars theatre.

II, ii, 11–12. Perhaps the Old Lady covers her ears with her hands and then uncovers them to ask if Bosola is still abusing women.

II, ii, 18–20. Since Jupiter came to her as a golden shower Danae was considered the type of a mercenary woman. *Cf.* I, ii, 168–9.

32 II, iii, 20–21. On the use of horoscopes for catching a thief and finding stolen goods, with particular reference to this passage, see Johnstone Parr, *Tamburlaine's Malady and Other Essays on Astrology in Elizabethan Drama* (Alabama, 1953), pp. 101–6.

34 II, iii, 56–63. For detailed comment on the exposition of the meaning of the horoscope see Johnstone Parr, *op. cit.*, pp. 94–100 and F. L. Lucas, *Webster*, ii, 153. Parr thinks that the horoscope indicates the futility of Delio's hope of establishing Antonio's son in his mother's right. (Delio apparently ignores the existence of the Duchess' eldest child who in fact ruled the dukedom of Amalfi from the Duchess' departure on the pilgrimage to Loretto in 1510 until his death in 1559.) Webster gives the horoscope the right details to indicate disaster, but these configurations did not occur at any time in the opening years of the sixteenth century. It may also be noted that as we think that Antonio Bologna did not return from France to Naples till early 1505, December 1505 should perhaps be the date given here. (The opening scene of the play makes it clear that Webster's Duchess has wasted no time in deciding to marry her newly-appointed major-domo.) See Gunnar Boklund, *op. cit.*, pp. 3–4.

II, iv. The scene opens with some tension as well as dramatic irony; for the audience knows that Castruchio has already left Amalfi for Rome. This and the following scene are set in the Cardinal's palace in Rome.

35 II, iv, 16–19: an anachronistic reference to the telescope constructed by Galileo in 1609 after he had heard of the one made by the Dutch spectacle-maker Nippershey.

II, iv, 33–36: the quality of the double entendre here indicates both the Cardinal's spiritual corruption and spiritual kinship with Ferdinand.

36 II, iv, 56–57. Julia teasingly equivocates with Delio so that he does not know whether she pities her husband's impotence or merely deplores its effect on herself.

37 II, v, 1–2. The mandrake, a plant of the genus Mandragora,

has a forked root and thus resembles the human form. It
was supposed to grow under the gallows and was said to
shriek when pulled from the ground. Moreover, plucking
it would lead to madness.

38   II, v, 12–13. Rhubarb, considered to be choleric itself, was
a recognized antidote for an excess of the choleric
humour.

II, v, 13. *here's the cursed day*, i.e. the horoscope, which
Bosola has enclosed in his letter.

39   II, v, 33, *the left side*, i.e. the wrong side. Vaughan refers
the reader to Sir Thomas Browne's *Pseudodoxia Epidemica*,
IV, 2 and quotes Ecclesiastes x, 2: 'A wise man's heart
is at his right hand; but a fool's heart is at his left.'
Lucas, (*Webster*, ii, 157) points out that the Hebrew
really means, 'A wise man's will is *for the right*; but a
fool's desire is *for the left*, i.e. tends in the wrong direction.' R. W. Dent, *op. cit.*, p. 201, quotes Matthieu's
*History of Lewis the Eleventh* (1614): 'The hearts of men
lie on the left side, they are full of deceit, Truth, free-
dome and loyalty are rare, vnknowne and exiled qualities.'
Dent says that the 'margin indicates Matthieu is being
both literal and figurative'. 'Left', in the sense of 'wrong'
is found in the Ulster phrase, 'He digs with the left
foot' meaning, 'He is of the wrong [religious] persuasion.'
*Cf.* III, i, 29 note.

40   III, i and ii. These scenes take place in the Duchess' palace
at Amalfi.

44   III, ii, 25–28. See Ovid, *Metamorphoses* I, 452; 689; XIV,
698.

46   III, ii, 69. It has been suggested that the Duchess catches
sight of Ferdinand in the mirror in front of which she
has been brushing her hair: see George Rylands, 'On
the Production of *The Duchess of Malfi*', a prefatory
essay to the Sylvan Press edition of the play (1945), p. ix.

48   III, ii, 146. *That gallery*. F. L. Lucas wonders if this means
that the Duke is 'meant to be visible to the audience while
crossing the upper stage, before he actually appears in the
Duchess' room' (*Webster*, ii, 165). I think it does; for the
audience's knowledge of Ferdinand's approach would give
the scene a tension similar to that of II, iv, thus under-
lining the parallel between the Duchess and Julia which
is emphasized in V, ii.

S.D. *she shows the poniard*. Since Antonio has already noticed
the poniard (1. 149) the direction implies that the
Duchess hands it to him for closer examination.

49    III, ii, 180. *Magnanima mensogna*. Lucas explains Webster's allusion here to Tasso's *Gerusalemne Liberata*, II, xxii, but R. W. Dent (*op. cit.*, p. 211) doubts that Webster was familiar with the work in either Italian or English.

49–    III, ii, 183–93. The equivocal language used by the Duchess
50    is a statement of her trust in Antonio and an explicit reminder to him of her wooing: III, ii, 187: *cf.* I, ii, 378–80.

51    III, ii, 243. *Pluto the god of riches*. Pluto, god of the underworld, was confused with Plutus, god of riches; probably through the idea of wealth coming from underground mines.

52    III, ii, 266. The Bermudas were famous for storms and had attracted particular attention after the shipwreck there of Sir George Summers, in 1609.

54    III, iii takes place in the Cardinal's palace in Rome.

56    III, iv and v. These scenes are set in Loretto.

57    III, iv, 9–14. In Q1 the last words of ll. 9, 10, 13 and 14 are hyphenated, thus indicating the fall of stress.

59    III, v, 33–39. Ferdinand's equivocation recalls the attitude of Shylock to Antonio's bond in *The Merchant of Venice* (IV, i, 223–6). It is noteworthy that Ferdinand's letter uses the same excuse to demand Antonio's presence that the Duchess gave for his dismissal: *cf.* III, ii, 166–70.

61    III, v, 79–80. Webster's source here is Donne's *An Anatomy of the World, The first Anniversary* ll. 155–7.

> Wee seem ambitious, Gods whole worke t'undoe;
> Of nothing hee made us, and we strive too,
> To bring our selves to nothing backe.

The change from 'God' to 'Heaven' may have been dictated to Webster by the requirements of the Lord Chamberlain, as G.P.V. Akrigg has suggested in 'The Name of God and *The Duchess of Malfi*', *Notes and Queries* CXCV (1950), 231–3. Other passages in which Akrigg thinks that Webster has had to substitute 'Heaven' for God are: I, ii, 393; II, v, 66; III, v, 77–8; III, v, 97; IV, ii, 217–18; V, iii, 40–41.

63    IV, i and ii. The fourth act is located 'Somewhere in Prison' (Lucas). In view of the conflicting evidence within the play itself (*cf.* III, v, 104; IV, i, 1–2; IV, ii, 367; V, ii, 121; V, iii, S.D., 1–2) one cannot and need not be more precise. See F. L. Lucas, *Webster*, ii, 177; M.C. Bradbrook, *Themes and Conventions of Elizabethan Tragedy* (Cambridge, 1935), pp. 14, 197.

**64**  IV, i, 39. *a sacrament o' th' Church*. Miss M. C. Bradbrook (*op. cit.*, p. 206) suggests that the Duchess is undergoing the sacrament of penance, but I feel that she refers here to her marriage, even though it was not celebrated in a church. *Cf.* Gunnar Boklund, *op. cit.*, p. 118.

IV, i, 43 S.D. A dead man's hand was a powerful charm used in the cure of madness. See M.C. Bradbrook, 'Two Notes upon Webster', *Modern Language Review* XLII (1947), pp. 283–84.

**65**  IV, i, 55 S.D. ANTONIO *and his children* Qq. If *children* is correct one assumes that Ferdinand wishes the Duchess to think that he has murdered the infant son and daughter imprisoned with her as well as the son who escaped with Antonio. In the following scene the Duchess gives instructions about these two (IV, ii, 200–202) which would suggest that she knows them to be alive. Miss M. C. Bradbrook thinks that these instructions proceed from Webster's desire to produce pathos by making the Duchess appear distractedly preoccupied with motherly concerns. (*Themes and Conventions of Elizabethan Tragedy*, p. 210.) Clifford Leech feels that an edge is given to the poignancy of the Duchess' maternal concern by 'her apparent, and extreme, lapse of memory'. (*Webster: 'The Duchess of Malfi'*, p. 22). The alternative suggested by some scholars is that the stage direction should be 'ANTONIO *and his child*'; but may we not simply assume that when the Duchess leaves the stage (IV, i, 109) she goes to another room where she finds the children still alive? Although the second scene obviously follows the first very quickly (as compared with the sequence of events in the first two acts) this does not necessarily mean that they both take place on the same day. (See *The Duchess of Malfi*, ed. F. L. Lucas (1958), p. 214, and Clifford Leech, *op. loc. cit.*)

**67**  IV, i, 113. *Vincentio Lauriola* has not been identified. See R. G. Howarth, 'Webster's Vincentio Lauriola', *Notes and Queries*, N.S. II (1955), 99–100.

IV, i, 117: *a penitential garment*. Bosola's suggestion perhaps implies that the Duchess should be punished as an adulteress. The sentence for adulteresses, passed by the ecclesiastical courts, was that they should walk through the streets in a penitential garment of white, carrying a lighted taper. So Jane Shore, in Heywood's *Second Part of King Edward the Fourth* (1599) appears in a white sheet, barefooted, with her hair about her ears, and in

CRITICAL NOTES

her hand a wax taper. *Cf.* Jessica's exclamation, 'What, must I hold a candle to my shames?' (*Merchant of Venice* II, vi, 41.)

68   IV, ii: Notable critical appreciations of this scene are to be found in: Charles Lamb, *Specimens of English Dramatic Poets, who lived About the Time of Shakespear: with notes* (1808), p. 217; S. I. Hayakawa, 'A Note on the madmen's scene in Webster's *The Duchess of Malfi*', *Publications of the Modern Language Association of America*, XLVII (1932), 907–9; C. W. Davies, 'The Structure of *The Duchess of Malfi*: An Approach', *English*, XII (1958), 89–93; Inga-Stina Ekeblad, 'The Impure Art of John Webster', *The Review of English Studies*, N.S. IX (1958), 253–67 (but see Gunnar Boklund, *op. cit.*, pp. 111–12; 182 n. 2).
     IV, ii, 26–27. *Cf.* Deuteronomy XXVIII, 15–34, and see M.C. Bradbrook, 'Two Notes upon Webster', p. 281.

69   IV, ii, 57. *transportation.* For the topical significance of this allusion see Lucas, *Webster*, ii, 182.

70   IV, ii, 92–93. The mad priest, who embodies a satirical portrait of a Jacobean Puritan parson (hence his description in Q4 actors' list), not of an early sixteenth-century Italian secular priest, is here referring to contemporary English versions of the Bible. As an extreme Puritan he disapproves of all save the Calvinistic Genevan Bible (*the Helvetian translation*) published in 1560. *Greek is turn'd Turk* implies that, in the Douay version of 1609–10 and the King James version of 1611 the Greek New Testament has turned Turk, i.e., become Moslem or infidel, by being put to the service of the wrong faith.

71   IV, ii, 113. *a soap-boiler costive.* This was the doctor's masterpiece because soap was used in suppositories to loosen, not bind, the bowels.

72   IV, ii, 133–8. These lines provide a bitter commentary on III, ii, 11–13; 58–60.
     IV, ii, 141–2. These lines are repeated verbatim from *The White Devil* V, i, 38–39. (Lucas's numbering.)
     IV, ii, 153–9. This is an allusion to a change in contemporary English styles in tombs which, F. L. Lucas suggests, may have come about through 'the Renaissance influence of Etruscan tombs with their effigies lying as at table'. (*Webster*, ii, 185.)

73   IV, ii, 170–1. The bellman rang his bell to attract attention for announcements of deaths and requests for prayers for the dead. In 1605 Robert Dowe of the Merchant Tailors'

Company gave an endowment to pay the clerk of St. Sepulchre's to toll the bell and go himself as bellman to exhort condemned prisoners in Newgate the night before their execution. Webster was born free of the Merchant Tailors' Company and his name is among the signatures to Dowe's endowment. As Dowe had died in 1612 the performance of this office would have been known to Webster's audience and therefore the dramatist could use the figure of the bellman to emphasize the fact that the Duchess has been, in a sense, condemned. (*Cf.* IV, ii, 294–8.)

IV, ii, 182. *Here your perfect peace is sign'd.* Peace in the sense of 'Quietus' would remind the Duchess of her own use of that term in I, ii, 377–80 and III, ii, 187. *Cf. Hamlet* III. i, 75–76.

IV, ii, 187–90. The Duchess is told that she must prepare her own body for burial; the implication being that there will be none to do that office for her after death. The reference to the crucifix suggests that there will be no priest to make the sign of the cross over her either. (In view of the significance of the use of the bellman's disguise, Gunnar Boklund is mistaken in thinking that Bosola refers here to the dressing of a bride: *op. cit.*, p. 112.)

74   IV, ii, 200–2: see note on IV, i, 55 S.D., p. 111 above.

IV, ii, 215–18. The basis of this striking image is the Virgilian 'Mille viæ mortis', which is also a Senecan commonplace. Webster could have found it in Montaigne or in Marston's *Antonio and Mellida.* The reference to the geometrical hinges which enable men to open the doors both ways is best interpreted as implying an antithesis between suicide and being murdered; 'the door swings two ways as far as the individual's grasp on life is concerned; it can be opened for him, or he can push it open himself'. (R. F. Whitman, 'Webster's "Duchess of Malfi" ', *Notes and Queries*, N.S. VI (1959), 174.) See also M. C. Bradbrook, *Themes and Conventions of Elizabethan Tragedy*, pp. 89–90; R. W. Dent, *John Webster's Borrowing*, p. 239; Clifford Leech, *Webster: 'The Duchess of Malfi'*, p. 44.

76   IV, ii, 269. *some sanctuary*, i.e. some place, such as a church, where, according to medieval ecclesiastical law, a fugitive from justice was entitled to immunity from arrest.

77   IV, ii, 282–4. It was the most distinguished member of the King's Men and probably the most famous Elizabethan

actor, Richard Burbage, who took the part of Ferdinand in early performances of the play. Later, according to the actors' list of Q1 and Q2, the part was taken by J. Taylor, who joined the King's Men in 1619, after Burbage's death.

78 IV, ii, 330. *Off my painted honour!* Bosola could be referring here to the fair appearance of the worldly position that he has gained through acting as Ferdinand's intelligencer: *cf.* V, ii, 292–3. G.V.P. Akrigg has suggested that ' "the painted honour" while "deceptive honour" can only refer to the hypocritical pretence of love for Ferdinand made in the lines immediately preceding'. ('A Phrase in Webster', *Notes and Queries*, CXCIII (1948), 454.) Comparison with V, ii, 300–1 strengthens this suggestion but, in fact, either or both interpretations may be accepted. See C. L. Barber, *The Idea of Honour in the English Drama, 1591–1700* (Gothenburg, 1957), p. 236.

IV, ii, 335 7: *cf. Othello* V, ii, 125–8.

IV, ii, 341. *So pity would destroy pity.* In calling for help, Bosola might only arouse Ferdinand who would prevent him from saving the Duchess.

79 IV, ii, 347. *Mercy.* This, as F. L. Lucas suggests, is probably 'a last half-conscious appeal to her murderers to spare her'. (*Webster*, ii, 189); *cf.* M. C. Bradbrook, *Themes and Conventions of Elizabethan Tragedy*, p. 208.

IV, ii, 360–2. These lines recall *3 Henry VI*, II, v, 61–72.

30 Act V takes place in Milan.

36 V, ii, 132–4. Not only is the Cardinal irreligious himself; he expects lesser churchmen to be like him, and as open to corruption as he is.

V, ii, 142. *Do, and be happy.* The Cardinal assumes that Bosola's previous words are spoken sarcastically, and so he answers in the same tone.

V, ii, 150 ff. Although this passage eases the dramatic tension by providing the audience with some comic relief as Bosola and Julia speak at cross-purposes, its structural function in the play is the presentation of an ironic parallel between Julia's wooing of Bosola and the Duchess' earlier wooing of Antonio. See Critical Introduction, pp. xxiii; xxiv-xxv.

86–87 V, ii, 151–5: *cf.* III, i, 63–69.

93 V, iii. 'This is perhaps the most purely moving scene the Duchess has.' (Charles Williams, 'On the Poetry of *The Duchess of Malfi*', Sylvan Press edition of the play (1945), p. xxi.) See also F. L. Lucas, *Webster*, ii, 195–6.

95 V, iv. One assumes that the main light on stage is provided

by candles or lanterns which the speakers hold: hence the
darkness and confusion when only one or two speakers
are present.

V, iv, 22–25: This is the clumsiest piece of dramaturgy in
the play: an intelligent audience does not need this
information.

96  V, iv, 42–45. If Bosola overhears Antonio's speech and takes
him for Ferdinand, he must think that Ferdinand (unlike
Hamlet) would kill a man when he is praying. In fact,
Antonio hopes that the Cardinal may reveal his otherwise
indiscernible Christian feelings after having been in
communion with God.

97  V, iv, 63–65. The image is not an echo of *King Lear* IV, i,
37–38; it is taken from an emblem found in Whitney's
*A Choice of Emblemes* (1586) and Hadrianus Junius's
collection of emblemata. (See Inga-Stina Ekeblad,
'Webster's "wanton boyes" ', *Notes and Queries*, N.S. II,
(1955), 294–5.)

98  V, v, 14–16. Bosola's refusal of wealth stresses the change in
his character and the strength of his determination.

99–  V, v, 48; 52. At first Ferdinand offers his adversary the
100  chance of being taken prisoner with the prospect of
being ransomed, but then he changes his mind and
decides not to grant 'the honour of arms' but press home
his advantage to the death.

101  V, v, 99–104; 119–20. Though some scholars (Moody E.
Prior, Ian Jack and Robert Ornstein, for example) see at
times, little or no connection between the play's sententiæ
and Webster's philosophy of life, Bosola's last words and
Delio's final couplet receive considerable attention in
discussions of the philosophy behind *The Duchess of
Malfi*. Interpretations of these passages vary considerably.
For example, Lord David Cecil devotes his essay on
Webster in *Poets and Storytellers* (1949), pp. 25–43, to an
appreciation of the Christian basis of Webster's morality,
while in 'The Case of John Webster', *Scrutiny* XVI, (1949),
38–43, Ian Jack sees the dramatist as an unbalanced
decadent, having no profound hold on any system of
moral values.

Interpretations of the play's philosophy which pay
particular attention to these two passages will be found
in: Una Ellis-Fermor, *The Jacobean Drama*, fourth
edition, revised (1958), pp. 170–3; 184–7 [first published
1936]; M. E. Prior, *The Language of Tragedy* (New York,
1947), pp. 132–5; Travis Bogard, *The Tragic Satire of*

CRITICAL NOTES

*John Webster* (Berkeley and Los Angeles, 1955), pp. 38–44; 141–5; S. L. Gross, 'A Note on Webster's Tragic Attitude', *Notes and Queries*, N.S. IV (1957), 374–5; C. G. Thayer, 'The Ambiguity of Bosola', *Studies in Philology*, LIV (1957), 162–71 [especially p. 171]; A. Kernan, *The Cankered Muse* (New Haven, Conn., 1959), pp. 240–2; J. R. Mulryne, ' "The White Devil" and "The Duchess of Malfi" ', *Stratford-upon-Avon Studies: 1 Jacobean Theatre* (1960), pp. 200–25 [especially pp. 216–17]; Robert Ornstein, *The Moral Vision of Jacobean Tragedy* (Madison, Wisconsin, 1960), pp. 130; 140–8; Irving Ribner, *Jacobean Tragedy: The Quest for Moral Order* (1962), pp. 105–6; 108–22; Gunnar Boklund, *'The Duchess of Malfi' Sources, Themes, Characters* (Cambridge, Mass., 1962), pp. 128–35; 164–70.

# TEXTUAL APPENDIX

*In collations and notes the following abbreviations are used:*
Q1—the edition of 1623 (British Museum copies: 644.f.72; Ashley 2207).
Q2—the edition of 1640 (British Museum copies: 82.c.26(3); 642.k.42).
Q3—the edition of 1678 (British Museum copy 163.k.65).
Q4—*The Unfortunate Dutchess of Malfy or The Unnatural Brothers* (1708) (British Museum copy 644.i.71).
Qq—all four quarto editions.
Q1a—uncorrected state of Q1.
Q1b—corrected state of Q1.
Q1c—second corrected state of Q1, found only in sheet G outer forme, i.e. in this edition: III, ii, 110–40; 201–73; III, iii, 2–31. Variant readings of Q1 are taken from the list given by Dr. J. R. Brown in 'The Printing of John Webster's Plays (II)', *Studies in Bibliography*, VIII (1956), 117–20.
Dyce—the revised edition (1857) of *The Works of John Webster*, edited by Alexander Dyce (1830).
Hazlitt—*The Dramatic Works of John Webster*, edited by W. C. Hazlitt (1857).
Vaughan—*The Duchess of Malfi*, edited by C. Vaughan, The Temple Dramatists (1896).
Sampson—*The White Devil* and *The Duchess of Malfi*, edited by Martin W. Sampson, The Belles Lettres Series (1904).
Brereton—J. le Gay Brereton, 'Webster's Twin Masterpieces', *Elizabethan Drama Notes and Studies* (Sydney, 1909) [an expanded version of his review, published in *Hermes* (1905), of Sampson's edition, with notes on readings and verse arrangement].
Lucas—*The Works of John Webster*, edited by F. L. Lucas, 4 vols. (1927).
McIlwraith—'The Duchess of Malfi', *Five Stuart Tragedies*, edited by A. K. McIlwraith, The World's Classics (1953).

*A—Collations and general notes on the text*

I, i. *Act I, Scene i* ed. Qq act and scene divisions are given in Latin.

[*Enter* ANTONIO *and* DELIO.] ed. Qq have 'block entries',
i.e. lists of all characters appearing in a particular scene.

I, i, 13. *in general* Q3, Q4 (Q1 ingenerall; Q2 in generall).
15. In Qq the reader's attention is directed to sententiæ
by quotation marks and/or the use of italics. In this
edition italics are used throughout.
19. *o'th'* ed. (Q1, Q2, Q3 oth'; Q4 [omits]).
34. *too much* Q2, Q3, Q4 (Q1 to-much).
44. *along* Q2, Q3, Q4 (Q1 a long).
49. *plum* Q1, Q2 (Q3, Q4 plumb).
53. *and* Q2, Q3, Q4 (Q1 an).
57. *died* Q1b (Q1a did).
58. *pardon* Q1b (Q1a pleadon).
66. *like* Q2, Q3, Q4 (Q1 likes).

I, ii, *Scene ii.* Although Qq give no indication of a clearing of
the stage at I, i, 81, 'SCENA II' is clearly marked, and
Antonio and Delio are included in the block entry for
the scene. Dyce first printed the act without the scene
division and other editors have followed him. [Sampson
makes a scene division later in the act.] An *Exeunt* after
I, i, 81 may have dropped out by accident, as an *Exit*
appears to have been omitted to indicate Bosola's leaving
the stage at II, iii, 76. If Antonio and Delio were intended
to leave the stage only to reappear again with the other
courtiers, it was presumably to give some impression of
the size of the Duchess' palace and of the two friends'
progress towards the presence chamber as they speak. If
they were intended to remain on stage, we may see them
pass through curtains (which are drawn back from
behind) from the outer to the inner stage for Scene ii.
Other courtiers will be found entering the inner stage
from the back or sides. Since the outer and inner stages
are used for Scene i and the early part of Scene ii respectively, there is no actual break in performance of Act I.
Nevertheless, there is no reason why a modern printed
edition of the play should not retain the scene division of
the quartos. (See J. R. Brown, 'The Printing of John
Webster's Plays (I)', *Studies in Bibliography*, VI (1954),
p. 132.)

I, ii, 7. *Antonio* Q3, Q4 (Q1, Q2 Antonia).
17. *do it* Q1, Q4 (Q2, Q3 to do it).
19. *as well* Q3, Q4 (Q1, Q2 as well).

27. *Ferdinand* ed. (Q1 *Fred.*; Q2, Q3, Q4 *Ferd.*).

36. *jennet* ed. (Q1, Q2 Gennit; Q3, Q4 Gennet).

45. *laugh when I laugh* Q1, Q2, Q3 (Q4 Not laugh but when I laugh).

78. *and one* Q1, Q2 (Q3, Q4 one).

84. *Flatterers* Q3, Q4 (Q1, Q2 Flatters).

94. *Twins?* Q1 (Q2, Q3, Q4 Twins).

110. *your* Q2, Q3, Q4 (Q1 you).

116. *Than your penance* Q1, Q2, Q3 (Q4 [omits]). Dyce, Hazlitt, Vaughan, Sampson, Lucas and McIlwraith accept this reading, though in his textual notes Lucas suggests the emendation 'And your penance'. In 'A Correction in Webster', *Notes and Queries*, CXCIII (1948), 302, J. C. Maxwell argues for the change to 'you', commenting that the meaning then becomes 'you will wish that she held it less vain-glory to talk much than you hold it penance to hear her'. This argument was accepted by Lucas for his revised reprint of the play in 1958, and the text was altered accordingly from that of the 1927 edition. The change seems to me unnecessary, since the lines as they stand may be interpreted as referring to the Duchess' excessive humility as well as her modesty : the qualities which make her auditors wonder. Thus, while acknowledging the vain glory of garrulousness, the Duchess is less distressed by that 'sin' than by the 'penance' (in the sense of punishment) she thinks she must be inflicting on those who have to listen to her.

127. *Antonio* Q2, Q3, Q4 (Q1 Antonia).

137. *let me entreat for* Qq.    Lucas suggests 'let me entreat for him'.

140. *We are now* Q4 (Q1 Wee now; Q2, Q3 We now; Dyce, Vaughan 'We [are] now'; Sampson, Lucas 'Wee [are] now'; Hazlitt 'We are now'; McIlwraith 'We now are'). The Q4 reading implies Ferdinand's haste to get the courtiers out of the way so that he may discuss his plans with the Cardinal.

143. *Duchess* ed. (Qq, Dyce, Hazlitt, Vaughan *Ferd.*) Sampson first pointed out that Ferdinand already knows that Silvio is going to Milan. If the Duchess asks the question Silvio's answer gives her the opportunity of offering to conduct him to the haven in her caroche.

147. *I have* Q1, Q2 (Q3 have I; Q4 have).

168. *Ferdinand* ed. (Q1 *Berd.*; Q2, Q3, Q4 *Ferd.*).

183. *thee* Q1, Q4 (Q2, Q3 three).

213. Sampson marks Scene ii here.

221. *pass'd* ed. (Qq. past).

226. *end* Q1, Q2, Q4 (Q3 ends).

227-8. Modernization of the Q1 punctuation produces two interpretations:
> (i) You live in a rank pasture here, i'th court: There is . . .
> (ii) You live in a rank pasture: here, i'th court There is a kind . . .

229. *to't* Q2, Q3, Q4 (Q1 too't).

238. *eaves* ed. (Q1a Eeues, Q1b Eues; Q2, Q3, Q4 Eves). Dyce modernized this as 'Eves', meaning 'evenings'; but, as F. L. Lucas points out, 'the primary sense is "eaves" (of which *eeves* and *eves* are merely variant spellings)'. *The Duchess of Malfi* (1958), p. 210.

243. *celebrated* Q2, Q3, Q4 (Q1 celibrated).

255. *women* Q2 (Q1 woemen; Q3 woman; Q4 [omits]).

284. *these triumphs* ed. (Q1, Q2 this triumphs; Q3, Q4 this triumph). Dyce emended to 'these triumphs' and his reading was followed by Hazlitt, Vaughan, Lucas and McIlwraith; Sampson read 'this triumph'.

290. *revenue* Q3, Q4 (Q1 reuinew; Q2 revenew).

302. *you* Q2, Q3, Q4 (Q1 yon).

309. *St. Winifred!* ed. (Qq, Sampson St. Winfrid). Dyce emended to 'Winifred'. The Welsh saint would be well known to English audiences. St. Winfred (or Wynfrith) was universally known as St. Boniface.

II, i, 33. *but you call it* Q3 (Q1, Q2 but you call; Q4 [omits]; Lucas 'but [I] call [it]'; McIlwraith 'No, no, but'). If 'you' is taken as the colloquial impersonal pronoun ( = one) Q3 reading may stand.

89. *out of fashion* Q2, Q3, Q4 (Q1 out off shashion).

118. *lemon peels* ed. (Q1 Lymmon pils; Q2 Lemmon pils; Q3 Lemon pills; Q4 Limon-peel). Sampson pointed out that the Q1 spelling could indicate 'pills' or 'peels' and Lucas confirmed that the reference here is to lemon peel, though his text preserves the Q1 spelling. It is probable that the waiting-woman would have scraps of peel, rather than manufactured pills, to sweeten her breath.

149. *a bett'ring of nature* ed. (Q1 a bettring . . .; Q2 bettring of . . .; Q3 bettering of . . .; Q4 bettering the Nature).

II, ii, 20. *Shut up* Q2, Q3, Q4 (Q1 Shht vp).

37. *Ha, ha, ha* Q2, Q3, Q4 (Q1 Hh, ha, ha).

57. *credibly* Q2, Q4 (Q1 creadably; Q3 credibily).

76. *Enter* CARIOLA *with a child* Q4 (Q1, Q2, Q3 [omit]).
If the birth were to be kept secret, it is strange to find
Cariola carrying the baby about the palace; but this
consideration is unlikely to have disturbed a Jacobean
audience. If the 'Three young Children', mentioned in
the Q1, Q2 actors' list, were not always available, a
'property baby' could be substituted for one child; and
it could be used later as the Duchess' youngest child,
referred to at III, v, 81.

II, iii, 9. *scream'd* ed. (Qq schream'd).

38–46. This passage, on Sig. E$_2$ of Q1, was set up by the
compositor who, of the two who worked on the play,
was the more likely to make mislineations, and two occur
between ll. 41–46. (See J. R. Brown, 'The Printing
of John Webster's Plays' (II) and (III), *Studies in
Bibliography*, VIII (1956), 123–7; XV (1962), 57–69.)
The prefix *Ant.* at ll. 38 and 40 suggests the loss of
something from Bosola. The assumption is supported
by the obscurity of ll. 40–41, which apparently refer to
Bosola's willingness to sign a copy of the horoscope as
proof of his desire to catch the thief and thus establish
his own innocence.

44. *wrought* Q1, Q2, Sampson, Lucas (Q3, Q4, Dyce,
Hazlitt, Vaughan, McIlwraith 'wrote'). The letters must
be embroidered in the handkerchief which Antonio
uses to stanch the blood from his nose. Had they
been written in the horoscope, Bosola would not have
had to look farther to identify the child's father.

50. *quit* Q3, Q4 (Q1, Q2 quite).

II, iv, 45. *tir'd* Q4 (Q1, Q2, Q3 tyr'd).

66. *seethe't* Dyce, Lucas (Q1, Q2 seeth's; Q3 seeth'd;
Q4 [changes sense]).

II, v, 20. *waste* Q2, Q3, Q4 (Q1 wast).

21. *honour's* ed. (Q1, Q2, Sampson, Lucas 'honors'; Q3,
Q4, Dyce, Hazlitt, Vaughan, McIlwraith 'honours'). The
honour to which Ferdinand refers here is the Duchess'
chastity and reputation for chastity, the damage to which
affects the honour of her whole family. Honour in this
sense is an uncountable, and so must here be in the geni-
tive, the meaning being 'as she has done the general
territory of her honour', i.e. her reputation and her

family's. See C. L. Barber, *The Idea of Honour in the English Drama* 1591–1700 (Gothenburg, 1957), p. 324 for the use of honour in the legal sense of 'a seignory of several manors held under one baron or lord paramount'. If this meaning (which was dying out) were intended, we would have to read 'honours''; but though Ferdinand complains of the Duchess' chargeable revels, we know that the real Duchess actually improved the economic position of the duchy, paying off the heavy debts that her first husband had incurred. (Lucas, *Webster*, ii, 8.)

56. *Yes, I can be angry* Qq, Sampson (Hazlitt 'Yes; I can be angry'; Lucas 'Yes—I can ...'; Dyce, Vaughan 'Yes [but] I can ...'; Brereton, McIlwraith 'Yes, yet I can ...').

57. *rupture* Qq. (Dyce queries possible reading 'rapture').

III, i, 27. *be* Q2, Q3, Q4 (Q1 he).
70. *horrid* Q3, Q4 (Q1, Q2 horred).
77. *by equivocation*, Q4 (Q1, Q2 (by equivocation; Q3 (by equivocation) ).
111. *then, pray?* Q2, Q3, Q4 (Q1 then? pray?).

III, ii, 16. *I pray thee Cariola* Q1, Q2, Q3 (Q4 I, prithee do Cariola). Sampson and Lucas retain the reading of Q1, Q2, Q3, but Dyce, Hazlitt, Vaughan and McIlwraith modernize (unnecessarily) to 'Ay, pray thee Cariola.' *Cf.* III, ii, 54.
25. *flight* Dyce *et al.* (Qq slight).
61. S.D. Q4 (Q1, Q2, Q3 [omit]).
71. *quickly* Q2, Q3, Q4 (Q1 quickle).
113. *tane* ed. (Q1a, Q3, Q4 ta'ne; Q1b, Q1c, Q2 taine).
   *massy* Q2, Q3, Q4 (Q1 massiy).
116. *name't* Q2, Q3 (Q1, Q4 nam't).
118. *too* Q2, Q3, Q4 (Q1 to).
124. *it was* Q1b, Q1c, Q2, Q3, Q4 (Q1a It was).
135. *shook* Q3, Q4 (Q1a, Q1b shooked; Q1c, Q2 shooke).
171. *Strange* Q2, Q3, Q4 (Q1 Srange).
176. *jewels* ed. (Q1 Iewlls; Q2, Q3, Q4 Jewels).
202. *As loth* Q1c (Q1a, Q1b A-loth).
203. *confiscate* Q1b, Q1c (Q1a confiffcate).
220. *those ... money* enclosed in brackets in Q1a, Q1b.
233. *Intelligencers* Q1c (Q1a, Q1b and Intelligencers).
235. *livery* ed. (Q1a, Q1b Liuory; Q1c Liuery).
238. *doom* Q3, Q4 (Q1a, Q1b doombe; Q1c, Q2 doome).
292. *In honour* Q2, Q3 (Q1 (In honour; Q4 "In honour).

THE DUCHESS OF MALFI

304. *Whither* Q3, Q4 (Q1, Q2 Whether).

326. *intelligencer* ed. (Q1 Intelligencer; Q2 Inteligencers; Q3, Q4 Intelligencers).

III, iii, 14. *He comes* Q1 (Q2 He come; Q3 He came; Q4 [omits]).

16. *be gone* Q3 (Q1 begon; Q2 be gon; Q4 [omits]).

III, v, 1. *Banish'd Ancona?* Qq, Sampson (Dyce, Hazlitt, Lucas, Vaughan, McIlwraith Banish'd Ancona!). The form of Antonio's answer and the Duchess' next query reinforce the impression that her opening words are not so much an exclamation as a question expressing bewilderment at what has happened. Moreover, we note that Q2, Q3 and Q4 retain the question mark where that of *Pity?* (III, v, 108), for example, is changed to an exclamation mark. *Cf. The White Devil* ed. J. R. Brown (1960), p. 7, on *The White Devil*, I, i, 1).

22. *the Lord Ferdinand; your brother*, As Lucas suggests, the semicolon here may imply a pause 'For there is indeed a distance between Ferdinand and brotherliness.' (*Webster*, ii, 207.)

31. *another* Q2, Q3, Q4 (Q1 annother).

72. The quotation mark indicating the importance of the line, which is here marked by the use of italics, was omitted in Q1a.

IV, i, 19. '*Pray-thee* Q1, Q2 (Q3 Pray-thee; Q4 Prithee).

74. *remember* Q1b (Q1a remembre).

IV, ii, 114. *too?* Q2, Q3 (Q1 to?; Q4 [omits]).

123. The punctuation of Q1 is equivocal, and could be modernized as either:
(i) Thou art a box of worm-seed; at best, but a . . .
or (ii) Thou art a box of worm-seed, at best; but a . . .

124. *cruded* Q1 (Q2, Q3, Q4 curded).

265. *agree* Q2, Q3, Q4 (Q1 ageee).

297. *judgment* Q2, Q3, Q4 (Q1 ludgment).

333. *were* Q2, Q3, Q4 (Q1 wete).

V, ii, 82. *too* Q2, Q3, Q4 (Q1 to).

113. *one* Q2, Q3, Q4 (Q1 on).

139. *brought* Q1, Q2, Q3 (Q4 [omits]). Sampson reads 'brought', but Dyce, Hazlitt, Vaughan and McIlwraith alter to 'bought'. Lucas reads '[bought]' but in his 1958 edition notes that picture makers might also be dealers to whom Antonio could sell a miniature of the Duchess.

Moreover, one has to assume that the Duchess' picture
was normally on sale in Milan (p. 215). One might add
that at this time Antonio still hopes to be reunited with
his wife and should, therefore, feel no need of a picture to
remind himself of her.

148 S.D. [*Enter* JULIA *with a pistol*] ed. The pistol is
suggested by ll. 158–9. Lucas reads [*Enter Julia, pointing
a pistol at him.*].

311. *off* Q3 (Q1, Q2 of; Q4 [omits]).

319. *rode* Q2, Q3, Q4 (Q1 rod).

V, iv, 11, *our* Q2, Q3, Q4 (Q1 out).

33. *quiet* Q2, Q3, Q4 (Q1 quiein).

60. *sad tidings* Qq. Brereton had 'a sort of suspicion that
we should read "glad tidings" '. (p. 15).

V, v, 50. *The devil?* Qq, Lucas (Dyce, Hazlitt, Sampson,
Vaughan and McIlwraith 'The devil!'). Retention of the
Qq ? implies Ferdinand's identification of the Cardinal
and the devil; alteration to ! turns his exclamation into a
curse. *Cf.* note on III, v, 1, above.

108. *too* Q2, Q3, Q4 (Q1 to).

B—*Variant readings which affect the verse structure of the play*

I, i, 31–33. Qq print as verse.

35–54 [. . . *leave me*] Qq print as verse.

54–61. Q1 prints as verse; Q2, Q3, Q4 print as prose.

62–68. Q1, Q2 print as verse; Q3, Q4 print as prose.

I, ii, 8–87. [. . . *Church,*] Qq print as verse.

87–89. Q1, Q2 print as verse; Q3, Q4 print as prose.

144. Sampson divides: . . . *down/To the haven.*

153–4. Qq, Lucas print as prose; Dyce, Hazlitt, Vaughan,
Sampson and McIlwraith print as verse.

155–6. Q1, Q2 print as prose; Q3, Q4 print as verse.

169–70. Qq, Dyce, Hazlitt, Vaughan, Sampson, Lucas
and McIlwraith print as one line. The division that I have
adopted is that suggested by J. R. Brown in 'The Printing
of John Webster's Plays—(III)', *Studies in Bibliography*
XV (1962), p. 63.

287b–8. Qq print as one line; Hazlitt divides: . . .
*excellence/. . . you:/. . . sake;/*; Dyce, Vaughan, Lucas and
McIlwraith divide: *Beauteous? | Indeed . . .*

289b–90. Qq divide: . . . *the/Particulars . . .*

309–10. Qq, Hazlitt, Sampson divide: ... *will.*/ ... *you*/
... *again.*/ Dyce and Vaughan read 'stranger' and divide
as Qq. Lucas and McIlwraith divide: ... *will*/ ...
*strange*/ ... *again.*/.

II, i, 1–47. Q1, Q2, Q3 and Hazlitt print as verse; Q4 cuts to
three lines.
64–66. Dyce and Vaughan print as prose.
80–84; 90–96; 99–110. Qq and Hazlitt print as verse.
119–20. Brereton and Lucas divide: ... *troubled*/*With* ...
121–2. Brereton divides: ... *say*/ ... *fore*/ ... *King.*/.
148–9. Qq, Sampson and Lucas divide: ... *pretty*/*Art*
...; Dyce, Hazlitt, Vaughan and McIlwraith divide:
*art,*/*This* ...

II, ii, 1–27. Qq and Hazlitt print as verse.
35–36. Qq divide: ... *Switzer*/*In* ...; Lucas and
McIlwraith divide: ... *even now*/*A Switzer* ...; Dyce,
Hazlitt, Vaughan and Sampson print as prose.
39–42. Qq, Lucas and McIlwraith print as verse; Dyce,
Hazlitt, Vaughan and Sampson print as prose.

II, iii, 40–41. Qq divide: ... *well, sir.*/*No, sir,*/ ... *to't.*/.
41b–42; 45–46. Qq print as one line.
44–48. Sampson divides: ... *name*/ ... *sir,*/ ... *safe.*/
... *lying-in.*/ ... *not.*/.

II, iv, 10c–11. Qq and Hazlitt print as one line.
68–69. Qq divide: ... *that,*/*To my* ...

II, v, 37. Qq, Dyce, Hazlitt and Vaughan print as two lines,
dividing: *Thus*/*Ignorance* ...
50–51. Qq divide: ... *rage!*/ ... *air*/.

III, i, 87–88. Qq, Dyce, Hazlitt and Vaughan divide: ... *are*/
*Your own* ...

III, ii, 14. McIlwraith divides: ... *like her*/*The better* ...
68–69. Q1, Q2, Q3 and Hazlitt print as one line; Q4, Dyce
*et al* divide: ... *tongue?*/'*Tis* ...
87–88. Qq divide: ... *I*/*Could* ...; Hazlitt divides:
*Yes,*/*If I* ...
151–2. Qq, Dyce, Hazlitt and Vaughan divide: ...
*uction*/*Seem'd* ...
153–4. Qq, Dyce, Hazlitt and Vaughan divide: ... *him,*/
*And so* ...

209–11. Q1, Q2 print as prose; Q3, Q4, Hazlitt and Brereton print as verse.

216–26. Qq print as verse; Brereton rearranges as verse.

266–8. Q1, Q2, Q3 print as two lines, dividing: ... *Politicians/* ... *heart string/*; Q4 [omits].

271–2. Qq, Dyce, Hazlitt and Vaughan divide: ... *fall/ Was* ...

312–14. Qq divide: ... *opinion/* ... *baths/* ... *Spa/*; Sampson divides: ... *hand./* ... *progress/* ... *Spa/*.

III, iii, 12–13a. Q1, Q2, Q3 print as one line; Dyce, Hazlitt, Vaughan, Sampson and McIlwraith print as prose; Q4 [omits]. I follow Lucas in accepting this as verse.

40–46. Qq print as verse, dividing: ... *scholar,/* ... *was in/* ... *beard was/* ... *tooth-ache,/* ... *know the/* ... *this/* ... *man./*. Hazlitt prints as verse, dividing: *scholar,/* ... *was in/* ... *beard was,/* ... *troubled/* ... *tooth-ache/* ... *know/* ... *this/* ... *man./*. Lucas rearranges the verse, dividing: ... *scholar/* ... *knots/* ... *was/* ... *tooth-ache/* ... *know/* ... *shoeing-horn,/* ... *did/* ... *man./*, but notes that the metre is 'very dubious'. Dyce, Vaughan, Sampson and McIlwraith print as prose.

50–52. Qq print as verse, dividing: ... *oppression/* ... *ones:/* ... *storm—/*; Lucas prints as verse, dividing: ... *oppression/* ... *ones/* ... *before/* ... *storm—/*; Dyce, Hazlitt, Vaughan, Sampson and McIlwraith print as prose.

54. Qq, Dyce, Hazlitt, Vaughan, Sampson and Lucas print as verse, dividing: ... *cannon/That.* ... McIlwraith prints as prose.

57–58. Qq, Hazlitt and Vaughan print as one line; Dyce and McIlwraith print as prose; Sampson and Lucas print as verse, dividing: ... *whisper/Their* ...

59b–61. Sampson and Lucas print 59b–60 as one line; but Qq divide 60–61: ... *fault, and/Beauty* ...; Hazlitt divides: *That, that* ... *her/Methinks* ... *beauty/*. I have followed the arrangement given by Dyce, Vaughan and McIlwraith.

III, v, 98–99. Qq and Hazlitt divide: ... *me/Whether* ...

105–6. Dyce, Vaughan and Sampson print three lines, dividing: ... *heard/* ... *o'er/* ... *again./*. McIlwraith has this division, but these are two and a half lines in his edition.

108–9. Q1, Q2, Q3 and Hazlitt print as one line; Q4 omits 109.

**IV, i,** 77–78. Qq and Sampson divide: ... *mend/The* ...;
Dyce, Hazlitt, Vaughan, Lucas and McIlwraith divide:
... *bee/When he* ...
94–95a. Dyce and Vaughan divide: ... *pray—/No,* ...
99b–100. Qq, Sampson, Lucas and McIlwraith print as
one line; Dyce, Vaughan and J. R. Brown (*op. loc. cit.*)
divide: ... *must/Remember* ...; Hazlitt divides: ...
*remember/My* ...
107–8. Qq and Hazlitt print as one line.

**IV, ii,** 37–38a. Qq, Dyce, Hazlitt, Vaughan and Sampson divide:
... *now!/What* ...; Brereton, Lucas and McIlwraith
divide: ... *tragedy./How* ...
83–113. Q1, Q2 print as verse; Q3, Q4 print as prose.
118–22. Lucas suggests the possible arrangement into
verse, dividing: ... *since/* ... *insensible/* ... *sure/* ... *I?/.*
123–31; 133–8. Q1, Q2 print as verse; Q3, Q4 print as
prose.
157–8. Qq divide: ... *their/Minds* ...; Hazlitt divides:
... *but/As* ...; Sampson, Lucas and McIlwraith divide:
... *but as/Their* ... Dyce and Vaughan print as prose.
357–9. In a note Sampson suggests the division: ...
*below/* ... *fountains/* ... *up/* ... *soul/* ... *father/.* Lucas
divides: ... *below/* ... *fountains/* ... *living?/.*
362–4. Qq print as two lines, dividing: ... *hence,/* ...
*deliver/*; Dyce, Hazlitt, Vaughan, Lucas and McIlwraith
divide: ... *Come,/* ... *hence,/* ... *deliver/*; Sampson
divides: ... *father./* ... *hence,/* ... *deliver/.*

**V, i,** 37b–38a. Brereton thinks that this should be one line.

**V, ii,** 30–32; 40–43; 47–51. Qq and Hazlitt print as verse.
53–54. Dyce and Vaughan print as prose.
55–56. Qq and Hazlitt divide: ... *mad/My* ...; Sampson,
Lucas and McIlwraith divide: ... *lord?/Are* ...; Dyce
and Vaughan print as prose.
57–61. Qq divide: ... *eye-/* ... *civil./* ... *him/* ...
*brought/* ... *you/*; Hazlitt divides: ... *off/* ... *civil./*
... *brought/* ... *you/*; Sampson and Lucas divide: ...
*eyebrows/* ... *civil./* ... *him/* ... *brought/* ... *you/*;
Dyce, Vaughan and McIlwraith pre/N prose.
65–66. Qq and Hazlitt divide: ... *me/Now* ...; Sampson
and Lucas divide: ... *begins/To* ...; Dyce, Vaughan and
McIlwraith print as prose.

68–80. Qq and Hazlitt print as verse.
164–5. Q1, Q2, Q3, Hazlitt and Sampson print as one line; Q4 [omits].
171c–2. Qq, Hazlitt and Lucas print as one line.
197–8. Q1, Q2, Q3 and Hazlitt print as one line; Q4 divides: ... *it.*/*The Cardinal* ...
205–6. Brereton says that these are really one line.
206–7. Dyce and Vaughan divide: ... *need*/*Follow* ...
227b–8. Sampson and McIlwraith print as one line.
231–4. Brereton rearranges the verse, dividing: ... *love*/ ... *it?*/ ... *when you*/ ... *suspect*/.
267–8. Qq divide: ... *your*/*Bosom* ...; Hazlitt divides: ... *you*/*Your* ...
270c–1. Qq and Hazlitt print as one line.
282–3. Qq and Hazlitt divide: ... *done,*/*I go,* ...
289–90. Qq print as one line; Hazlitt divides: ... *me*/*For* ...
297. Qq, Hazlitt, Sampson and Lucas divide: ... *more,*/*There is* ...; Dyce, Vaughan and McIlwraith divide: ... *there is*/*A Fortune* ...
310–15. Qq and Hazlitt print as verse.
316–18. Dyce and Vaughan divide: ... *remove*/ ... *out*/ ... *inquiry*/ ; Lucas divides: ... *me*/ ... *body*/ ... *plague*/. I retain the Qq arrangement, as do Hazlitt, Sampson and McIlwraith.
320. Brereton would divide: ... *Naples*/*To take* ...

V, iii, 33–34. Brereton retains the Q1, Q2, Q3 reading 'passes' and divides: ... *passes*/*of*/*Your* ...

V, iv, 35–37. Dyce, Vaughan and Sampson print as prose.
42b–43. Qq, Dyce, Hazlitt, Vaughan and Sampson divide: ... *prayers*/*There* ... I follow the division suggested by Brereton and adopted by Lucas and McIlwraith.
66–68. Brereton would divide: ... *good*/ ... *preparative*/ ... *ask*/*The* ...
70–71. Lucas suggests the division: ... *son*/*Fly* ...

V, v, 7–8. Qq and Hazlitt print as one line; Dyce, Vaughan' Sampson and McIlwraith divide: ... *come?*/*Thou* ... Lucas divides: ... *me.*/*Now? art* ...
12–13. Brereton thinks this should be one line.
16b–17. Qq, Dyce, Hazlitt, Vaughan and Sampson print as one line. I follow the division of Brereton, Lucas and McIlwraith.

33–35. Qq and McIlwraith print as two lines, dividing:
... *door*/ *To* ...; Lucas prints as two lines, dividing: ...
*unbarracade*/ *The* ...
55–61. Q1, Q2 and Hazlitt print as verse; Q3, Q4 print as
verse to ... *prosperity*/ and give the rest of the speech in
prose.
68b–69. Qq and Hazlitt print as one line.